T0207481

Communications
in Computer and Information Science   1990

Editorial Board Members

Joaquim Filipe ⓘ, *Polytechnic Institute of Setúbal, Setúbal, Portugal*
Ashish Ghosh ⓘ, *Indian Statistical Institute, Kolkata, India*
Raquel Oliveira Prates ⓘ, *Federal University of Minas Gerais (UFMG),*
Belo Horizonte, Brazil
Lizhu Zhou, *Tsinghua University, Beijing, China*

Rationale

The CCIS series is devoted to the publication of proceedings of computer science conferences. Its aim is to efficiently disseminate original research results in informatics in printed and electronic form. While the focus is on publication of peer-reviewed full papers presenting mature work, inclusion of reviewed short papers reporting on work in progress is welcome, too. Besides globally relevant meetings with internationally representative program committees guaranteeing a strict peer-reviewing and paper selection process, conferences run by societies or of high regional or national relevance are also considered for publication.

Topics

The topical scope of CCIS spans the entire spectrum of informatics ranging from foundational topics in the theory of computing to information and communications science and technology and a broad variety of interdisciplinary application fields.

Information for Volume Editors and Authors

Publication in CCIS is free of charge. No royalties are paid, however, we offer registered conference participants temporary free access to the online version of the conference proceedings on SpringerLink (http://link.springer.com) by means of an http referrer from the conference website and/or a number of complimentary printed copies, as specified in the official acceptance email of the event.

CCIS proceedings can be published in time for distribution at conferences or as post-proceedings, and delivered in the form of printed books and/or electronically as USBs and/or e-content licenses for accessing proceedings at SpringerLink. Furthermore, CCIS proceedings are included in the CCIS electronic book series hosted in the SpringerLink digital library at http://link.springer.com/bookseries/7899. Conferences publishing in CCIS are allowed to use Online Conference Service (OCS) for managing the whole proceedings lifecycle (from submission and reviewing to preparing for publication) free of charge.

Publication process

The language of publication is exclusively English. Authors publishing in CCIS have to sign the Springer CCIS copyright transfer form, however, they are free to use their material published in CCIS for substantially changed, more elaborate subsequent publications elsewhere. For the preparation of the camera-ready papers/files, authors have to strictly adhere to the Springer CCIS Authors' Instructions and are strongly encouraged to use the CCIS LaTeX style files or templates.

Abstracting/Indexing

CCIS is abstracted/indexed in DBLP, Google Scholar, EI-Compendex, Mathematical Reviews, SCImago, Scopus. CCIS volumes are also submitted for the inclusion in ISI Proceedings.

How to start

To start the evaluation of your proposal for inclusion in the CCIS series, please send an e-mail to ccis@springer.com.

Boris Shishkov · Andon Lazarov
Editors

Telecommunications and Remote Sensing

12th International Conference, ICTRS 2023
Rhodes, Greece, September 18–19, 2023
Proceedings

 Springer

Editors
Boris Shishkov
Institute of Mathematics and Informatics
Bulgarian Academy of Sciences
Sofia, Bulgaria

University of Library Studies
and Information Technologies
Sofia, Bulgaria

IICREST
Sofia, Bulgaria

Andon Lazarov
Nikola Vaptsarov Naval Academy
Varna, Bulgaria

K.N. Toosi University of Technology
Tehran, Iran

ISSN 1865-0929   ISSN 1865-0937 (electronic)
Communications in Computer and Information Science
ISBN 978-3-031-49262-4   ISBN 978-3-031-49263-1 (eBook)
https://doi.org/10.1007/978-3-031-49263-1

© The Editor(s) (if applicable) and The Author(s), under exclusive license
to Springer Nature Switzerland AG 2023

This work is subject to copyright. All rights are reserved by the Publisher, whether the whole or part of
the material is concerned, specifically the rights of translation, reprinting, reuse of illustrations, recitation,
broadcasting, reproduction on microfilms or in any other physical way, and transmission or information
storage and retrieval, electronic adaptation, computer software, or by similar or dissimilar methodology now
known or hereafter developed.
The use of general descriptive names, registered names, trademarks, service marks, etc. in this publication
does not imply, even in the absence of a specific statement, that such names are exempt from the relevant
protective laws and regulations and therefore free for general use.
The publisher, the authors, and the editors are safe to assume that the advice and information in this book
are believed to be true and accurate at the date of publication. Neither the publisher nor the authors or the
editors give a warranty, expressed or implied, with respect to the material contained herein or for any errors
or omissions that may have been made. The publisher remains neutral with regard to jurisdictional claims in
published maps and institutional affiliations.

This Springer imprint is published by the registered company Springer Nature Switzerland AG
The registered company address is: Gewerbestrasse 11, 6330 Cham, Switzerland

Paper in this product is recyclable.

Preface

We are witnessing huge technical and technological progress in telecommunications, concerning satellite communication technologies, mobile communication systems, advanced networking, and so on. Next to that, we observe impressive developments in remote sensing, concerning advanced sensing technologies and sensor networks. This allows for: (i) full-value context awareness in servicing users, such that the service is adapted to the user's location and situation; (ii) powerful navigation of ground, water, and aerial vehicles; (iii) advanced real-time collaborations across countries and regions. All this combines with advanced software technologies and artificial intelligence to allow for really effective automated information and communication servicing of users and society. At the same time, there are huge societal implications to be considered, such as public values (safety, privacy, accountability, and so on), authority/responsibility issues, ethics, and so on. This brings us together at ICTRS, the International Conference on Telecommunications and Remote Sensing, inspired by the work of Blagovest Shishkov who established and led the ICTRS conference series until he passed away in 2015.

This book contains the proceedings of ICTRS 2023 – the 12th edition of the conference, held in Rhodes, Greece and online, during September 18–19, 2023 (https://www.ictrs.org). ICTRS is an annual event that brings together researchers and practitioners interested in the above-mentioned topics.

Since the first event took place in Sofia, Bulgaria, in 2012, we have enjoyed 11 successful ICTRS editions. The conference has been held in different European countries (Bulgaria, The Netherlands, the Grand Duchy of Luxembourg, Greece, Italy, and Spain) but took place virtually in 2020 and 2021. This year's edition brought ICTRS back to where the 2015 and 2019 editions took place – Rhodes, Greece.

The high quality of the ICTRS 2023 technical program was enhanced by informal discussion on drone technology, following on from those in previous years. These, and other discussions, helped to stimulate community building and facilitated possible R&D project acquisition initiatives, which definitely contributes to maintaining the event's high quality and inspiring our steady and motivated community.

The ICTRS 2023 Program Committee consisted of 40 members from 17 countries (Australia, Brazil, Bulgaria, Canada, France, Germany, Greece, Iran, Ireland, Italy, Japan, The Netherlands, Russia, Spain, Turkey, the UK, and the USA, listed alphabetically) – all of them competent and enthusiastic representatives of prestigious organizations.

In organizing ICTRS 2023, we have observed high ethical standards: we guaranteed at least three reviews per submitted paper (assuming reviews of adequate quality), under the condition that the paper fulfilled the ICTRS 2023 requirements. In assigning a paper for review, it was our responsibility to provide reviewers who had the relevant expertise. Sticking to a double-blind review process, we guaranteed that a reviewer would not know who had (co-)authored the paper (we sent anonymized versions of the papers to the reviewers) and that an author would not know who had reviewed his/her paper. We required reviewers to respect the content of the paper and not disclose (parts of) its content to third parties before the conference (and also after the conference in case of rejection). We guarded against conflicts of interests by not assigning papers to reviewers who were immediate colleagues of any of the co-authors. Further, in our decisions to accept/reject papers, we also guarded against discrimination based on age, gender, race, or religion. Finally, with regard to the EU data protection standards, we followed the GDPR requirements.

For the 12th consecutive year, ICTRS maintained a high scientific quality whilst providing a stimulating collaborative atmosphere.

With ICTRS essentially focusing on telecommunications and remote sensing plus relevant societal implications, ICTRS 2023 has addressed many research areas and topics which, as can be seen from the proceedings, included the following main directions: image/signal analysis and processing; electronics and photonics; cryptography; effects on human health concerning telecommunications and remote sensing; societal impacts of telecommunications and remote sensing, particularly in relation to public values and renewable-energy-related applications. Also, as in previous ICTRS editions, several papers have addressed applicability-related issues that concern pilotless vehicles in general, and drones in particular.

ICTRS 2023 received 24 paper submissions, from which 11 papers were selected for publication in the current proceedings. Of these papers, 7 full papers were selected for 30-minute oral presentations at the conference. The ICTRS 2023 chairs and authors hail from Bulgaria, Canada, Germany, Greece, Iran, Kazakhstan, The Netherlands, and Russia (listed alphabetically).

ICTRS 2023 was organized and sponsored by the Interdisciplinary Institute for Collaboration and Research on Enterprise Systems and Technology (IICREST), with the cooperation of Delft University of Technology (TU Delft), Aristotle University of Thessaloniki (AUTH), and AMAKOTA Ltd. Further, the ICTRS editions are held under the auspices of the International Union of Radio Science (URSI).

Organizing this interesting and successful conference required the dedicated efforts of many people. Firstly, we must thank the authors whose research and development achievements are recorded here. Next, the Program Committee members each deserve credit for their diligent and rigorous peer reviewing. Further, we would like to mention the excellent organization provided by the IICREST team (especially Canka Petrova and Aglika Bogomilova) and the support extended by AMAKOTA Ltd.; the ICTRS 2023 organizers did all the necessary work to deliver a stimulating and productive event, and we have to acknowledge the valuable support from our colleagues from Delft and Thessaloniki. Last but not least, we are grateful to Springer for their willingness to publish the ICTRS 2023 proceedings and we thank the editorial team for their professionalism and patience (regarding the preparation of the proceedings).

We wish you inspiring reading! We look forward to meeting you next year for the 13th International Conference on Telecommunications and Remote Sensing (ICTRS 2024), details of which will be made available at https://www.ictrs.org.

October 2023

Boris Shishkov
Andon Lazarov

Organization

General Co-chairs

Marijn Janssen — Delft University of Technology, The Netherlands

Boris Shishkov — Institute of Mathematics and Informatics, Bulgarian Academy of Sciences/ULSIT/IICREST, Bulgaria

Program Co-chairs

Andon Lazarov — Nikola Vaptsarov Naval Academy, Bulgaria and K.N. Toosi University of Technology, Iran

Dimitris Mitrakos — Aristotle University of Thessaloniki, Greece

Program Committee

Catherine Algani	CNAM, France
Mauro Assis	National Institute for Space Research and URSI, Brazil
Vera Behar	Institute for Information and Communication Technologies, Bulgarian Academy of Sciences, Bulgaria
Maurice Bellanger	CNAM, France
Jun Cheng	Doshisha University, Japan
Yoshiharu Fuse	Japan Space Systems, Japan
Ivan Garvanov	ULSIT, Bulgaria
Marijn Janssen	Delft University of Technology, The Netherlands
Hristo Kabakchiev	Sofia University St. Kliment Ohridski, Bulgaria
Kazuya Kobayashi	Chuo University, Japan
Mohamed Latrach	ESEO, France
Frank Little	Texas A&M University, USA
Marco Luise	University of Pisa, Italy
Olga Maktseva	Southern Federal University, Russia
Andrea Massa	University of Trento, Italy
Wolfgang Mathis	Leibniz Universität Hannover, Germany
Lyudmila Mihaylova	Lancaster University, UK

Tomohiko Mitani	Kyoto University, Japan
Tadao Nagatsuma	Osaka University, Japan
Shoichi Narahashi	NTT Docomo, Inc., Japan
Elizabeth Nuncio	Fraunhofer Institute for High Frequency Physics and Radar Technologies, Germany
Mairtin O'Droma	University of Limerick, Ireland
Takashi Ohira	Toyohashi University of Technology, Japan
Yoshiharu Omura	Kyoto University, Japan
Jaques Palicot	CentraleSupélec, France
Brent Petersen	University of New Brunswick, Canada
Hermann Rohling	Hamburg University of Technology, Germany
Sana Salous	Durham University, UK
Hamit Serbest	Cukurova University, Turkey
Naoki Shinohara	Kyoto University, Japan
Boris Shishkov	Institute of Mathematics and Informatics, Bulgarian Academy of Sciences/ULSIT/IICREST, Bulgaria
Alexander Shmelev	Academician A. L. Mints Radiotechnical Institute, Russia
Jun-ichi Takada	Tokyo Institute of Technology, Japan
Hiroyuki Tsuji	National Institute of Information and Communications Technology, Japan
Marten van Sinderen	University of Twente, The Netherlands
Christos Verikoukis	Telecommunications Technological Centre of Catalonia, Spain
Julian Webber	ATR, Japan
Satoshi Yagitani	Kanazawa University, Japan
Tsuneki Yamasaki	Nihon University, Japan
Zhenyu Zhang	University of Southern Queensland, Australia

Contents

Full Papers

ISAR Imaging Algorithm Based on Fourier Dictionary Signal
Decomposition and L0 Norm Minimization 3
  Andon Lazarov and Dimitar Minchev

Probability Characteristics of CFAR Processors in Presence of Randomly
Arriving Impulse Interference 17
  Ivan Garvanov

Influence of Advance Time on Accuracy of the Ionospheric Total Electron
Content Forecast 33
  Olga A. Maltseva and Artem M. Kharakhashyan

A Public-Key System Based on Primes and Addition 51
  Rodney H. Cooper, Jeff Retallick, and Brent R. Petersen

Objects Detection in an Image by Color Features 65
  Georgi Tsonkov and Magdalena Garvanova

Telecommunications and Remote Sensing: A Public Values Perspective 77
  Boris Shishkov and Magdalena Garvanova

Integrated Platform for Vehicle Charging Based on Renewable Energy
Resources 90
  Radostin Dolchinkov, Atanas Yovkov, Velizar Todorov,
  and Kristian Ventsislavov

Short Papers

Acoustic System for the Detection and Recognition of Drones 107
  Ivan Garvanov, Penka Pergelova, and Nurym Nurdaulet

A Study on Thermal Influence on Adolescents Due to Long-Term Mobile
Phone Exposure 117
  Georgi Tsonkov, Gabriela Garvanova, and Daniela Borissova

Vibrations in Ships and Crew Health 127
  Kolyo Oreshkov, Radoslav Simionov, Kamen Seymenliyski,
  Radostin Dolchinkov, Silvia Letskovska, and Eldar Zaerov

x   Contents

A Review of Pilotless Vehicles 136
  Boris Shishkov and Gabriela Garvanova

Author Index 145

Full Papers

Full Papers

ISAR Imaging Algorithm Based on Fourier Dictionary Signal Decomposition and L0 Norm Minimization

Andon Lazarov[1,2]([✉]) and Dimitar Minchev[3]

[1] Information Technologies Department, Nikola Vaptsarov Naval Academy, Varna, Bulgaria
a.lazarov@naval-acad.bg
[2] K.N, Toosi University of Technology, Tehran, Iran
[3] Burgas Free University, Burgas, Bulgaria
mitko@bfu.bg

Abstract. In In the present work an Inverse Synthetic Aperture Radar (ISAR) image reconstruction algorithm based on Fourier Dictionary signal decomposition and l_0 norm minimization of the image matrix is suggested. Three-dimensional (3-D) ISAR geometry and kinematics are analytically described. An ISAR signal model based on Stepped Frequency Modulation (SFM) waveform is derived. An original steepest ascent algorithm is created with a Gaussian function increasing maximal pixel intensities and decreasing pixel intensities of low level. Simulation experiments prove the effectiveness of the developed algorithm.

Keywords: ISAR imaging · ISAR signal Fourier decomposition · 2-D l0 norm minimization

1 Introduction

ISAR is the microwave technology for detection, tracking and imaging of objects moving in free space under all weather conditions and visibility at different times of the day. Two-dimensional images of the observed objects with azimuth and range coordinates are extracted from the highly informative wide-spectrum microwave signals reflected by the object applying non-parametric and parametric methods [1–6].

Special phase compensating and focusing algorithms are applied to improve image quality. In the case of a limited number of geometrically defining scattering points, the compressed sensing technique and norm minimization algorithms are applied [7–18].

ISAR imaging includes the following stages - high order motion compensation and focusing, rang and azimuth compression. For maneuvering targets, classical phase autofocus algorithms cannot compensate high order phases induced by high order target's maneuvering motion, which leads to the blurring of ISAR images. To solve this problem, an iterative phase autofocus approach for ISAR imaging of maneuvering targets is proposed in [1].

Accurate translational motion compensation is the key procedure of inverse synthetic aperture radar imaging. In case of sparse aperture, the correlation of adjacent pulses is

© The Author(s), under exclusive license to Springer Nature Switzerland AG 2023
B. Shishkov and A. Lazarov (Eds.): ICTRS 2023, CCIS 1990, pp. 3–16, 2023.
https://doi.org/10.1007/978-3-031-49263-1_1

destroyed, which affects translational motion compensation and imaging. A translational motion compensation technique for ISAR imaging is proposed in [2], where joint phase adjustment and ISAR imaging is established.

A phase adjustment and full-aperture reconstruction for sparse aperture ISAR imaging of maneuvering targets is discussed in [4], where a modified eigenvector-based autofocus approach is applied to correct phase errors within sparse aperture measurements of maneuvering targets, and after phase correction, the full aperture data are reconstructed from sparse aperture measurements via sparse representation under a redundant chirp-Fourier dictionary.

Sparse aperture applied in inverse synthetic aperture radar (ISAR) imaging affects the image quality obtained by a traditional range Doppler (RD) algorithm as well as translational motion compensation, while focusing. To reduce influence of motion errors on the target imaging, reweighted alternating direction method of multipliers is proposed in [5] to realize the joint processing of phase adjustment and ISAR imaging.

An effective method to achieve translational motion compensation for maneuvering targets with sparse aperture is proposed in [6], where the translational and rotational motions are approximated by cubic polynomial and quadratic polynomial, respectively.

A sparse recovery algorithm applied to a radar signal model with missing observed RCS data samples, based on the compressive sensing, for the formulation of the radar signatures, such as high-resolution range profile and ISAR image is presented in [7].

Comparison performance analysis of sparse recovery algorithms (SRAs) including the basis pursuit (BP), the BP de-noising, and the orthogonal matching pursuit for the reconstruction of a 2-D inverse synthetic aperture radar (ISAR) image from incomplete radar-cross-section (RCS) data is provided in [8]. In [9] is evaluated the classification accuracy of inverse synthetic aperture radar images extracted trough the conventional Fourier transform (FT) and sparse recovery algorithms based on compressive sensing (CS) from incomplete radar cross section (RCS) data.

In [10], an autofocus method is presented aimed to achieve high-resolution ISAR image reconstruction with limited measurements by compressive sensing (CS) approach combined with Tikhonov-regularization-based algorithm as an effective focusing technique. An algorithm based on compressed sensing has been developed in [11], that integrates range alignment and phase correction step to the iteration loop of an Iterative Shrinkage and Threshold Algorithm.

In [12] a 3D near-field sparse SAR direct imaging algorithm for irregular trajectories, adopting a piece of preliminary information in the SAR image to update the dictionary matrix dimension, using the Gaussian iterative method, and optimizing the signal-processing techniques, which can achieve 3D sparse reconstruction in a more direct and rapid manner.

Based on cubic polynomial and quadratic polynomial description of the translational and rotational motions, an effective method to achieve translational motion compensation for maneuvering targets with sparse aperture is suggested in [13]. Based on the amplitude identical Laplace probability distribution of the target scattered field follows an identical Laplace probability distribution, a super-resolution algorithm for forming ISAR images from limited observations is developed in [14].

In [15] an iterative l0 algorithm based on compressed sensing is proposed to estimate and compensate the phase errors and reconstruct a high-resolution focused image from limited pulses. A computer mathematical model based on Single Instruction, Multiple Data (SIMD) physical machine model combined with parallel computing mathematical modeling as SAR/ISAR signal formation and image processing is discussed in [16]. Sparse decomposition of two dimensional signals and compressive sensing–based algorithm for passive bistatic ISAR with DVB-T signals are considered in [17, 18].

The goal of the present work is to develop an ISAR image reconstruction algorithm based on a Fourier dictionary decomposition of the ISAR signal matrix and sparse distribution of scattering points on the object's surface. In contrast to many algorithms based on the minimization of the l0 norm of the ISAR image matrix [6–17], in the present work an original steepest ascent algorithm to minimize l0 norm of the ISAR image matrix is suggested.

The rest of the paper is organized as follows. In Section II, 3D ISAR geometry and object's kinematics are described/.In Section III, stepped frequency modulation waveform and ISAR signal modeling are discussed. In Section IV, ISAR signal image reconstruction based on l0 norm minimization realized by steepest ascent procedure is presented. In Section V, results of the numerical experiments are provided. In Section VI, conclusion remarks are given.

2 3-D Geometry and Kinematics of ISAR Scenario

Consider a three-dimensional (3-D) object presented by a 3-D regular grid of reference points in a Cartesian system $O'XYZ$. The object is moving in a coordinate system of observation $Oxyz$ on rectilinear trajectory at a constant vector velocity $\mathbf{V}$ (Fig. 1). The geometric center of the 3-D object, the origin of 3-D coordinate grid, and the origin of the coordinate system $O'XYZ$ coincide. The reference points are placed at each node of the 3-D grid and are used to describe the shape of the object. The current distance vector $\mathbf{R}_{ijk}(p) = \left[x_{ijk}(p), y_{ijk}(p), z_{ijk}(p)\right]^T$ measured from ISAR, placed in the origin of the coordinate system $Oxyz$ to the ijk th reference point from the object space, is determined by the vector equation

$$\mathbf{R}_{ijk}(p) = \mathbf{R}_{0'}(p) + \mathbf{AR}_{ijk}, \tag{1}$$

where $\mathbf{R}_{0'}(p) = \left[x_{0'}(p), y_{0'}(p), z_{0'}(p)\right]^T$ is the current distance vector of the object geometric center defined by the expression $\mathbf{R}_{0'}(p) = \mathbf{R}_{0'}(0) + \mathbf{V}.T_p.p$, where $p = \overline{0, N-1}$ is the number of the emitted pulse, N is the full number of emitted pulses, $\mathbf{R}_{0'}(0) = \left[x_{0'}(0), y_{0'}(0), z_{0'}(0)\right]^T$ is the distance vector to the geometric center of the object space at the moment of the first emitted pulse, $p = 0$, T_p is the pulse repetition period, $\mathbf{V} = [V.\cos\alpha, V.\cos\beta, V.\cos\delta]^T$ is the vector velocity. $\mathbf{R}_{ijk} = \left[X_{ijk}, Y_{ijk}, Z_{ijk}\right]^T$ is the distance vector to the ijk th reference point in the coordinate system $O'XYZ$; $X_{ijk} = i(\Delta X)$, $Y_{ijk} = j(\Delta Y)$ and $Z_{ijk} = k(\Delta Z)$ are the discrete coordinates of the ijk-th reference point in the coordinate system $O'XYZ$; ΔX, ΔY and ΔZ are the spatial dimensions of the 3-D grid cell; $\cos\alpha$, $\cos\beta$ and $\cos\delta = \sqrt{1 - \cos^2\alpha - \cos^2\beta}$ are the guiding cosines and V is the module of the vector velocity. The indexes, i, j, k are uniformly spaced in the coordinate axes, $O'X$, $O'Y$, $O'Z$. In ISAR scenario description the point A with a position vector, $\mathbf{R}_{ijk}$ is a reference point from the object space, the point $O'(0)$ with coordinates $x_{O'}(0)$, $y_{O'}(0)$, $z_{O'}(0)$ is the origin of the coordinate system $O'XYZ$ of the object, the position of the geometric center at the moment $p = 0$.

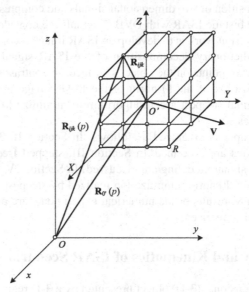

Fig. 1. A 3-D ISAR geometry and kinematics

The elements of the transformation matrix $\mathbf{A}$ in Eq. (1) are determined by the Euler expressions

$$a_{11} = \cos \psi \cos \phi - \sin \psi \cos \theta \sin \phi;$$
$$a_{12} = - \cos \psi \sin \phi - \sin \psi \cos \theta \cos \phi;$$
$$a_{13} = \sin \psi \sin \theta;$$
$$a_{21} = \sin \psi \cos \phi + \cos \psi \cos \theta \sin \phi; \quad a_{31} = \sin \theta \sin \phi;$$
$$a_{22} = - \sin \psi \sin \phi + \cos \psi \cos \theta \cos \phi; \quad a_{32} = \sin \theta \cos \phi;$$
$$a_{23} = - \cos \psi \sin \theta; \quad a_{33} = \cos \theta. \tag{2}$$

Angles ψ, θ and ϕ define the space orientation of the 3D coordinate grid, where the object is depicted. The module of the ijk-th scattering point's position vector, $\mathbf{R}_{ijk}(p)$ is defined by equation

$$\left| \mathbf{R}_{ijk}(p) \right| = \left[(x_{ijk}(p))^2 + (y_{ijk}(p))^2 + (z_{ijk}(p))^2 \right]^{\frac{1}{2}}. \tag{3}$$

Expression (3) can be used to calculate the time delay of signals reflected from the object's scattering points while modelling an ISAR signal.

3 Stepped Frequency Waveform and ISAR Signal Model

Stepped Frequency Waveform

The target is illuminated by series of SFM bursts modeled by the following expression

$$s(t) = \sum_{p=1}^{N} \sum_{m=0}^{M-1} \text{rect} \frac{t - t_{mp}}{T_b} \exp[j2\pi f_m] \qquad (4)$$

where

$$\text{rect} \frac{t - t_{mp}}{T_b} = \begin{cases} 1, & 0 < \dfrac{t - t_{mp}}{T_b} \leq 1; \\ 0, & \dfrac{t - t_{mp}}{T_b} < 0 \text{ and } \dfrac{t - t_{mp}}{T_b} > 1; \end{cases} \qquad (5)$$

$f_m = f_0 + m\Delta f$ is the frequency of the pulse centered at time t_{mp}, defined by $t_{mp} = mT + p.T_p$, and for pulses spaced equally in frequency and time domain; Δf is the pulse frequency difference in the burst; T_b is the burst time width; M is the number of pulses in each burst; $p = \overline{0, N-1}$ - the burst index; T is the pulse time width in the burst period of the pulses in the burst), T_p is the burst repetition period.

ISAR Signal Model

Denote a_{ijk} as a reflectivity coefficient of the moving target scattering point. The ISAR signal reflected by the target scattering point for a single mth pulse frequency f_m and p-th burst is defined by

$$\hat{s}_{ijk}(m, p) = \text{rect}\left(\frac{t - t_{ijk}(p)}{T_b}\right).a_{ijk}.\exp\left[j2\pi f_{m-r}(t - t_{ijk}(p)\right] \qquad (6)$$

where

$$\text{rect}\left(\frac{t - t_{ijk}(p)}{T_b}\right) = \begin{cases} 1, & \text{if } 0 \leq \dfrac{t - t_{ijk}(p)}{T_b} < 1; \\ 0, & \text{otherwise} \end{cases} \qquad (7)$$

where $t = t_{ijk\,\min}(p) + m.T$ is the current fast time initialized by the time delay from nearest stationary scattering point, $t_{ijk\,\min}(p)$; $f_{m-r} = f_0 + (m - r)\Delta f$ is the frequency of each pulse in the burst; n is the current number of the frequency pulse; $r = m$, where r is the number of the frequency pulse equal m, when the signal reflected by the ijk-th scattering point from the moving target is detected; $t_{ijk}(p) = \frac{2R_{ijk}(p)}{c}$ is the time delay of the ISAR signal reflected by the object's scattering point with intensity a_{ijk}, where c is the speed of light. The value $R_{ijk}(p)$ is the module of the distance vector from ISAR to the object's scattering point. The coordinates of the ijk-th object's scattering point at the p th moment are calculated by the matrix equation

$$\begin{bmatrix} x_{ijk}(p) \\ y_{ijk}(p) \\ z_{ijk}(p) \end{bmatrix} = \begin{bmatrix} x_{O'}(0) + V_x.p.T_p \\ z_{O'}(0) + V_y.p.T_p \\ z_{O'}(0) + V_z.p.T_p \end{bmatrix} - \begin{bmatrix} a_{11} & a_{12} & a_{13} \\ a_{21} & a_{22} & a_{23} \\ a_{31} & a_{32} & a_{33} \end{bmatrix} \cdot \begin{bmatrix} X_{ijk} \\ Y_{ijk} \\ Z_{ijk} \end{bmatrix}. \qquad (8)$$

The ISAR signal from the object can be modeled by the expression

$$\hat{s}(m, p) = \sum_{ijk} \mathbf{rect}\left(\frac{t - t_{ijk}(p)}{T_b}\right) . a_{ijk} . \mathbf{exp}\left[j2\pi f_{m-r}(t - t_{ijk}(p))\right], \quad (9)$$

where $t = t_{ijk\,\min}(p) + m.T$ is the current fast time, $t_{ijk\,\min}(p) = \frac{2R_{ijk\,\min}(p)}{c}$ is the minimum time delay from the nearest scattering point.

$$\mathbf{rect}\left(\frac{t - t_{ijk}(p)}{T_b}\right) = \begin{cases} 1, & \text{if } 0 \le \dfrac{t - t_{ijk}(p)}{T_b} < 1; \\ 0, & \text{otherwise} \end{cases} \quad (10)$$

The demodulation of the ISAR signal is performed by its multiplication with a complex conjugated emitted waveform.
$\exp\left[-j2\pi (f_0 + (m - r)\Delta f)t\right]$, which yields

$$\hat{s}_D(m, p) = \sum_{ijk} \mathbf{rect}\left(\frac{t - t_{ijk}(p)}{T_b}\right) . a_{ijk} . \mathbf{exp}\left[-j2\pi f_{m-r}(t_{ijk}(p))\right] \quad (11)$$

The exponential term in (11) can be presented as a multiplication of two exponential terms, i.e.

$$.\exp[-j2\pi f_{m-r} . t_{ijk}(p)]$$
$$= \exp[-j2\pi f_0 . t_{ijk}(p)] . \exp[-j2\pi (m - r)\Delta f . t_{ijk}(p)] \quad (12)$$

The first term is modified as

$$\exp[-j2\pi f_0 . t_{ijk}(p)] = \exp\left[-j\left(\frac{2\pi . p . \hat{p}}{N} + \Phi(p)\right)\right], \quad (13)$$

where $\hat{p} = \frac{f_D}{\Delta f_D}$ is the Doppler index, $f_D = \frac{2.f_0 R_{ijk}{}'(0)}{c}$ is the Doppler frequency, $R_{ijk}{}'(0)$ is the first derivative of $R_{ijk}(p)$ at the moment of imaging $p = 0$, $\Delta f_D = \frac{1}{N.T_p}$ is the Doppler resolution defined by the full observation period, $\Phi(p)$ is the phase term of a higher order.

The second term in (13) is presented as

$$\exp[-j2\pi (m - r)\Delta f . t_{ijk}(p)] = \exp\left[-j\frac{2\pi . k . \hat{k}}{M}\right], \quad (14)$$

where $k = m - r$ is the frequency range index, $\hat{k} = \frac{R_{ijk}(p)}{\Delta R}$ is the spatial range index, $\Delta R = \frac{c}{2\Delta F}$ is the range resolution dimension, $\Delta F = M.\Delta f$ is the frequency bandwidth of the emitted waveform, In case all pulses reflected from the target are registered, substitute $m - r = k, k = \overline{0, M - 1}$ is the range sample index, $\Delta f = \frac{\Delta F}{M}$ is the pulse frequency difference, ΔF is stepped frequency pulse bandwidth.

Then, the SAR signal model (11) can be rewritten as

$$\hat{s}_D(k, p) = \sum_{\hat{k},\hat{p}} a_{\hat{k},\hat{p}} \cdot \exp\left[-j\left(\frac{2\pi.p.\hat{p}}{N} - \Phi(p)\right)\right] \cdot \exp\left[-j\frac{2\pi.k.\hat{k}}{M}\right], \qquad (15)$$

where the rectangular function is omitted based on assumption that all signals from scattering point are registered ($m = r$), and three dimensional image function a_{ijk} is reduced to two dimensional $a_{\hat{k},\hat{p}}$. The indices $\hat{k}, \hat{p}$ define the sctering points coordinates at the moment of imaging.

4 ISAR Image Reconstruction Technique

ISAR Signal Sparse Decomposition

Expression (15) can be considered as a decomposition of the ISAR signal in a 2-D discrete Fourier basis. At the first stage assume that $\Phi(p, k) = 0$. In matrix form the (15) can be written as [17, 18]

$$\mathbf{S} = \mathbf{P}.\mathbf{A}.\mathbf{K}^T, \qquad (16)$$

where $\mathbf{S}(N \times K)$ is the measurement signal matrix, $\mathbf{P}(N \times \hat{N})$ is the cross-range matrix-dictionary, $\mathbf{K}(K, \hat{K})$ is the range matrix dictionary, $\mathbf{A}(\hat{N} \times \hat{K})$ is the image matrix.

Define $\mathbf{P}$ and $\mathbf{K}$ as vector-rows of vectors as follows

$$\mathbf{P} = [\mathbf{p}_1, \mathbf{p}_2, \mathbf{p}_3,..., \mathbf{p}_{\hat{p}}, ..., \mathbf{p}_{\hat{N}}] \qquad (17)$$

$$\mathbf{K} = [\mathbf{k}_1, \mathbf{k}_2, \mathbf{k}_3,..., \mathbf{k}_{\hat{k}},..., \mathbf{k}_{\hat{K}}] \qquad (18)$$

$$\mathbf{p}_{\hat{p}} = \left[\mathbf{exp}(j2\pi.\hat{p}/\hat{N}), \mathbf{exp}(j2\pi.2.\hat{p}/\hat{N}), ., \mathbf{exp}(j2\pi.N.\hat{p}./\hat{N})\right]^T \qquad (19)$$

$$\mathbf{k}_{\hat{k}} = \left[\mathbf{exp}(j2\pi.\hat{k}/\hat{K}), \mathbf{exp}(j2\pi.2.\hat{k}/\hat{K}), ., \mathbf{exp}(j2\pi.N.\hat{k}./\hat{K})\right]^T \qquad (20)$$

The expression (16) denotes two-dimensional discrete Fourier decomposition of the signal in matrix form. It means that the two-dimensional signal $\mathbf{S} \in \mathbf{R}^{N \times K}$ is decomposed as linear combination of atoms $\mathbf{\Psi}_{p,k}$, where $p = \overline{1, N}, k = \overline{1, K}$), i.e.

$$\mathbf{S} = \sum_{\hat{p}=1}^{\hat{N}} \sum_{\hat{k}=1}^{\hat{K}} a(\hat{p}, \hat{k})\mathbf{\Psi}_{\hat{p},\hat{k}} \qquad (21)$$

where $\mathbf{\Psi}_{\hat{p},\hat{k}} = \mathbf{p}_{\hat{p}}\mathbf{k}_{\hat{k}}^T$.

In case $N = \hat{N}$ (complete measurement) the decomposition (16) is unique, it means that there exists a unique sparsest solution for $\mathbf{A}$. In over complete case $N' < \hat{N}$(the number of cross-range signal measurements N' is less the number of scattering points on that direction $\hat{N}$), and $K' < \hat{K}$(the number of range signal measurements K' is less the number of scattering points on that direction $\hat{K}$), i.e. $\mathbf{X} \in \mathbf{R}^{N' \times K'}$ over the redundant Fourier dictionaries $\mathbf{P} \in \mathbf{R}^{N \times \hat{N}}$ and $\mathbf{K} \in \mathbf{R}^{K \times \hat{K}}$, the decomposition of $\mathbf{X}$ is not unique. The compressed measurement matrix $\mathbf{X}(N' \times K')$ can be obtained by matrix multiplication with two Gaussian identity sensing matrices of the left and right parts in Eq. (16), i.e.

$$\mathbf{\Phi}_p.\mathbf{S}.\mathbf{\Phi}_k^T = \mathbf{\Phi}_p.\mathbf{P}.\mathbf{A}.\mathbf{K}^T.\mathbf{\Phi}_k^T \tag{22}$$

where $\mathbf{\Phi}_p(N' \times N)$ and $\mathbf{\Phi}_k(K' \times K)$ are sensing Gaussian matrices with one non-zero entry in each row of the matrices.

Denote $\mathbf{X} = \mathbf{\Phi}_p.\mathbf{S}.\mathbf{\Phi}_k^T + \mathbf{W}$, the compressed measurement (sensed) matrix defined by sensing. Gaussian identity matrices and measurement matrix signal, where $\mathbf{W}$ is the white Gaussian noise matrix, $\hat{\mathbf{P}} = \mathbf{\Phi}_p.\mathbf{P}$ and $\hat{\mathbf{K}}^T = \mathbf{K}^T.\mathbf{\Phi}_k^T$ are reduced matrices-dictionary. The image reconstruction problem can be solved by definition of sparse decomposition of the measurement signal

$$\mathbf{min}\|\mathbf{A}\|_0 \text{ subject to } \left\|\mathbf{X} - \hat{\mathbf{P}}.\mathbf{A}.\hat{\mathbf{K}}^T\right\|_2^2 \leq \varepsilon, \tag{23}$$

where $\mathbf{min}\|\mathbf{A}\|_0$ is the l_0- norm that denotes the number of non-zero scattering point intensities in image matrix $\mathbf{A}$, that means to find out the image matrix $\mathbf{A}$ with as much zero entries as possible, $\left\|\mathbf{X} - \hat{\mathbf{P}}.\mathbf{A}.\hat{\mathbf{K}}^T\right\|_2^2$ denotes the square of the Euclidian norm, ε is a small constant.

ISAR Imaging Algorithm Based on l_0 Norm Minimization

1. Calculate the initial estimate of the image matrix $\hat{\mathbf{A}}_0$ [17].
   $\hat{\mathbf{A}}_0 = \hat{\mathbf{P}}^*.\mathbf{X}.(\hat{\mathbf{K}}^*)^T$, which corresponds to an initial variance $\sigma_0 = \infty$,
   where $\hat{\mathbf{P}}^* = \hat{\mathbf{P}}^T(\hat{\mathbf{P}}.\hat{\mathbf{P}}^T)^{-1}$, $\hat{\mathbf{K}}^* = \hat{\mathbf{K}}^T(\hat{\mathbf{K}}.\hat{\mathbf{K}}^T)^{-1}$ are the pseudo-inverses of $\hat{\mathbf{P}}$ and $\hat{\mathbf{K}}$, respectively.
2. Define the next value of the variance $\sigma_1 = (2-4).(\max|\hat{a}_{\hat{p},\hat{k}}|)$ where $(\max|\hat{a}_{\hat{p},\hat{k}}|)$ is the maximum absolute value of an entry in the matrix $\hat{\mathbf{A}}_0$.
3. Define decreasing sequence of variances as $\sigma_1 > \sigma_2 > ... > \sigma_j > ... > \sigma_J$, where $\sigma_j = c.\sigma_{j-1}, 0.5 \leq c \leq 1$.
4. For a fixed σ_j maximize the function $F_\sigma(\mathbf{A}) = \sum_{\hat{p},\hat{k}} \exp\left(-\frac{\hat{a}_{\hat{p},\hat{k}}^2}{2\sigma_j^2}\right)$, $\hat{p} = \overline{1, \hat{N}}, \hat{k} = \overline{1, \hat{K}}$
   by steepest ascent algorithm followed by projection onto the feasible set onto the feasible set $\left\{\mathbf{A}\Big|\mathbf{X} = \hat{\mathbf{P}}.\mathbf{A}.\hat{\mathbf{K}}^T\right\}$ in $l = 1, ..., L$ iterations. Maximization of $F_\sigma(\mathbf{A})$ means increasing the number of zeros entries in the image matrix $\mathbf{A}$.

Steepest Ascent Algorithm with an Exponential Gaussian Function
Initialization:
   For $\sigma = \sigma_j$, $\mathbf{A} = \hat{\mathbf{A}}_{j-1}$, where $j = \overline{1, J}$.

1. Set $j = 1$, then $\sigma = \sigma_1$, $\mathbf{A} = \hat{\mathbf{A}}_0$. Set $l = 1$.

   a. Calculate the matrix $\boldsymbol{\Delta} = [\delta_{\hat{p},\hat{k}}]$,

   where $\delta_{\hat{p},\hat{k}} = \exp\left(-\dfrac{\hat{a}_{\hat{p},\hat{k}}^2}{2\sigma_j^2}\right)$, where $\hat{a}_{\hat{p},\hat{k}} \in \hat{\mathbf{A}}_0, \hat{p} = \overline{1, \hat{N}}, \hat{k} = \overline{1, \hat{K}}$.

2. Calculate the corrected image matrix $\hat{\mathbf{A}}_{0\prime} = \hat{\mathbf{A}}_0 - \mu\boldsymbol{\Delta}$, where $\mu \geq 1$ is a positive constant (for smaller value of σ, smaller values of μ should be applied).

3. Project the matrix $\hat{\mathbf{A}}_0$ back onto the feasible set, by the following expression [17]
$$\hat{\mathbf{A}}_0^{\prime\prime} = \hat{\mathbf{A}}_0^{\prime} - \hat{\mathbf{P}}^*(\hat{\mathbf{P}}.\hat{\mathbf{A}}_0^{\prime}.\hat{\mathbf{K}}^T - \mathbf{X})(\hat{\mathbf{K}}^*)^T \text{ where } \mathbf{X} = \hat{\mathbf{P}}.\hat{\mathbf{A}}_0.\hat{\mathbf{K}}^T.$$

4. Set $l = 2$, Substitute $\hat{\mathbf{A}}_0 = \hat{\mathbf{A}}_0^{\prime\prime}$, then $\hat{\mathbf{A}}_{0\prime} = \hat{\mathbf{A}}_0 - \mu\boldsymbol{\Delta}$,
$$\hat{\mathbf{A}}_0^{\prime\prime} = \hat{\mathbf{A}}_0^{\prime} - \hat{\mathbf{P}}^*(\hat{\mathbf{P}}.\hat{\mathbf{A}}_0^{\prime}.\hat{\mathbf{K}}^T - \mathbf{X})(\hat{\mathbf{K}}^*)^T \text{ where } \mathbf{X} = \hat{\mathbf{P}}.\hat{\mathbf{A}}_0.\hat{\mathbf{K}}^T.$$

5. Set $l = 3$. Substitute $\hat{\mathbf{A}}_0 = \hat{\mathbf{A}}_0^{\prime\prime}$, then $\hat{\mathbf{A}}_{0\prime} = \hat{\mathbf{A}}_0 - \mu\boldsymbol{\Delta}$,
$$\hat{\mathbf{A}}_0^{\prime\prime} = \hat{\mathbf{A}}_0^{\prime} - \hat{\mathbf{P}}^*(\hat{\mathbf{P}}.\hat{\mathbf{A}}_0^{\prime}.\hat{\mathbf{K}}^T - \mathbf{X})(\hat{\mathbf{K}}^*)^T, \text{ where } \mathbf{X} = \hat{\mathbf{P}}.\hat{\mathbf{A}}_0.\hat{\mathbf{K}}^T.$$

6. Set $l = l$. Substitute $\hat{\mathbf{A}}_0 = \hat{\mathbf{A}}_0^{\prime\prime}$ defined on $(l-1)$-th step, then $\hat{\mathbf{A}}_{0\prime} = \hat{\mathbf{A}}_0 - \mu\boldsymbol{\Delta}$,
$$\hat{\mathbf{A}}_0^{\prime\prime} = \hat{\mathbf{A}}_0^{\prime} - \hat{\mathbf{P}}^*(\hat{\mathbf{P}}.\hat{\mathbf{A}}_0^{\prime}.\hat{\mathbf{K}}^T - \mathbf{X})(\hat{\mathbf{K}}^*)^T \text{ where } \mathbf{X} = \hat{\mathbf{P}}.\hat{\mathbf{A}}_0.\hat{\mathbf{K}}^T. \text{ Repeat calculation } L$$
times until $\hat{\mathbf{A}}_0^{\prime\prime} = \hat{\mathbf{A}}_0^{\prime}$, i.e. $\hat{\mathbf{A}}_0^{\prime\prime}$ does not change.

7. Set $j = j$, $\sigma = \sigma_j$, and $\hat{\mathbf{A}}_0 = \hat{\mathbf{A}}_{j-1}^{\prime\prime}$, go to step 1, a and repeat the procedure.

8. Final solution $\hat{\mathbf{A}}_0 = \hat{\mathbf{A}}_J$.

5 Simulation Experiment

To verify the properties of the developed 3-D model of ISAR trajectory signal with stepped frequency modulation and to prove the correctness of the l_0 image reconstruction procedure a numerical experiment is carried out. It is assumed that the target is moving rectilinearly in a 3-D Cartesian coordinate system of observation $Oxyz$. The trajectory parameters are: the module of the vector velocity $V = 300$ m/s; $\alpha = \pi$; $\beta = \pi/2$; $\gamma = \pi/2$. The coordinates of the target mass-center at the moment $p = 0$: $x_{00}(0) = 3.10^4$ m; $y_{00}(0) = 1, 5.10^4$ m; $z_{00}(0) = 3.10^3$ m. ISAR signal parameters are: wavelength is $\lambda = 3$ cm., SFM burst timewidth is $T = 1$ ms., SFM pulse number is $M = 512$, carrier frequency is $f = 10$ GHz., SFM pulse timewidth is $\Delta T = 7.81$ μs., SFM total bandwidth is $\Delta F = 0.15$ GHz., SFM bursts number emitted during inverse aperture synthesis is $N = 512$. The frequency difference between frequency pulses in the burst is $\Delta f = 1.17$ MHz. The 2-D MiG29 sparse image matrix of size $[128 \times 128]$ is presented in Fig. 2.

The real (a) and imaginary (b) parts of the 2-D complex ISAR signal, of full size $[512 \times 512]$ are depicted in Fig. 3.

The real (a) and imaginary (b) parts of the 2-D complex ISAR signal of reduced size $[128 \times 128]$ are depicted in Fig. 4.

The real (a) and imaginary part of the complex ISAR image $\hat{\mathbf{A}}_0$ of MiG29 extracted by 2-D Fourier transform of the sparse ISAR signal is presented in Fig. 5.

The MiG29 complex ISAR image, amplitude (a) and phase (b) extracted by 2D Fourier transform from the sparse ISAR signal is presented in Fig. 6.

The ISAR amplitude image (a) obtained by 2-D Fourier transform and reconstructed ISAR amplitude image (b) by applying l_0 norm minimization of the ISAR image matrix

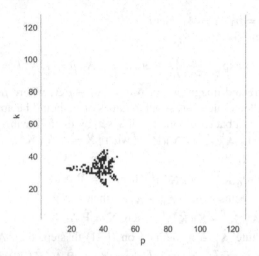

Fig. 2. A 2D sparse image of the aircraft MiG29

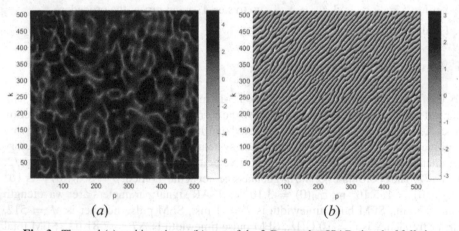

(a) (b)

Fig. 3. The real (a) and imaginary (b) part of the 2-D complex ISAR signal of full size

and steepest ascent algorithm is presented in Fig. 7. The ISAR image in Fig. 7, a is characterized with low contrast. The ISAR image in Fig. 7, b is characterized with higher contrast achieved by the steepest ascent algorithm with an exponential Gaussian function that increases maximal pixel intensities and decreases low pixel intensities.

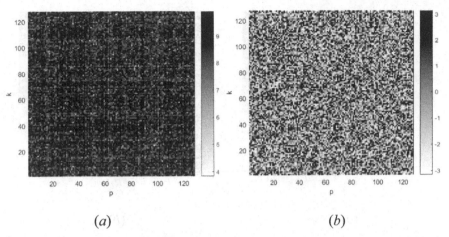

(a) (b)

Fig. 4. The real (a) and imaginary (b) parts of the 2-D complex ISAR signal of reduced size [128 × 128]

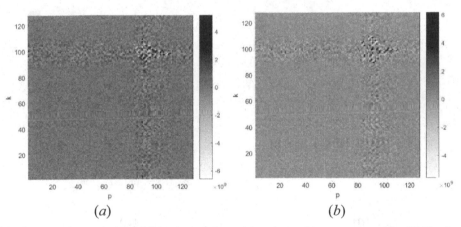

(a) (b)

Fig. 5. MiG29 complex ISAR image, real (a) and imaginary (b) part extracted by 2D Fourier transform from the sparse ISAR signal.

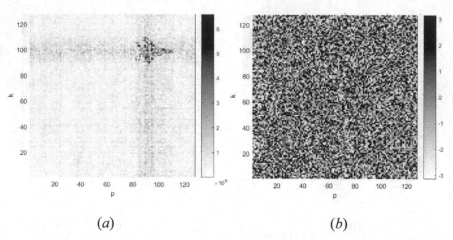

(a)   (b)

Fig. 6. MiG29 complex ISAR image, amplitude (a) and phase (b) extracted by 2D Fourier transform from the sparse ISAR signal

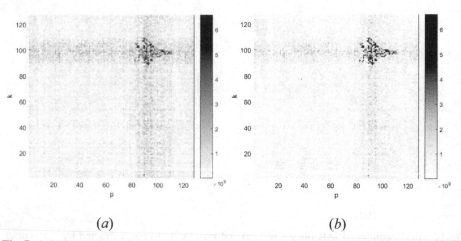

(a)   (b)

Fig. 7. MiG29 ISAR image extracted by 2-D Fourier transform (a) and from the sparse ISAR signal by applying l_0 norm minimization and a steepest ascent algorithm (b)

6 Conclusion

In the present work 3-D ISAR geometry and kinematics are analytically described. A SFM ISAR signal model is derived. An image reconstruction algorithm based on Fourier dictionary decomposition of ISAR signal and 2-D l_0 norm minimization of the ISAR image matrix is developed. An original steepest ascent algorithm based on Gaussian function minimizing l_0 norm of the ISAR image matrix is created. Results of simulation experiments are provided to prove the correctness and effectiveness of the developed image reconstruction algorithm.

Acknowledgment. This research was funded by Bulgarian National Science Fund (BNSF), under project grant number KP-06-N57/6, entitled "Theoretical and experimental research of models and algorithms for formation and control of specific relief textures on different types of functional surfaces". This research is also supported by National Scientific Program – Security and Defence adopted by Decision of the Council of Ministers No. 731 of October 21, 2021.

References

1. Wang, B., et al.: An iterative phase autofocus approach for ISAR imaging of maneuvering targets. Electronics **10**(17), 2100 (2021). https://doi.org/10.3390/electronics10172100
2. Wei, X., Yang, J., Lv, M., Chen, W., Ma, X.: Translational mtion compensation for ISAR imaging based on range joint fast orthogonal matching pursuit algorithm. IEEE Access **10**(2022), 37382–37395 (2022)
3. Wei, J., Shao, S., Ma, H., Wang, P., Zhang, L., Liu, H.: High-resolution ISAR imaging with modified joint range spatial-variant autofocus and azimuth scaling, 2020. Sensors **20**(18), 5047 (2020). https://doi.org/10.3390/s20185047
4. Zhang, L., Duan, J., Qiao, Z.-J., Xing, M.-D., Bao, Z.: Phase adjustment and ISAR imaging of maneuvering targets with sparse apertures. China IEEE Trans. AES **50**(3) (2014)
5. Wei, X., Yang, J., Lv, M., Chen, W., Ma, X.: A reweighted alternating direction method of multipliers for joint phase adjustment and ISAR imaging. Remote Sens. Lett. **13**, 1020–1028 (2022)
6. Liu, F., Huang, D., Guo, X., Feng, C.: Translational Motion compensation for maneuvering target echoes with sparse aperture based on dimension compressed optimization. IEEE Trans. Geosci. Remote Sens. **60**, 1–16 (2022). https://doi.org/10.1109/TGRS.2022.3169275
7. Bae, J.-H., Kim, K., Yang, E.: A study on the formulation of high resolution range profile and ISAR image using sparse recovery algorithm. J. Korean Inst. Electromagn. Eng. Sci. **25**(4), 467–475 (2014). https://doi.org/10.5515/KJKIEES.2014.25.4.467
8. Bae, J.-H., Kang, B.-S., Kim, K.-T., Yang, E.: Performance of sparse recovery algorithms for the reconstruction of radar images from incomplete RCS data. IEEE Geosci. Remote Sens. Lett. **12**(4), 860–864 (2015). https://doi.org/10.1109/LGRS.2014.2364601
9. Lee, S.-J., Bae, J.-H., Kang, B.-S., Kim, K.-T., Yang, E.-J.: Classification of ISAR images using sparse recovery algorithms. In: 2014 IEEE Conference on Antenna Measurements and Applications (CAMA), Antibes Juan-les-Pins, France, pp. 1–4 (2014). https://doi.org/10.1109/CAMA.2014.7003316
10. Kang, M.-S., Kim, K.-T.: Compressive sensing approach for high-resolution ISAR image reconstruction and autofocus, Wiley, October 2019. J. Eng. **6** (2019). https://doi.org/10.1049/joe.2019.0572
11. Rosebrock, F., Rosebrock, J., Cerutti-Maori, D., Ender, J.: ISAR imaging by integrated compressed sensing, range alignment and autofocus. In: EUSAR 2021; 13th European Conference on Synthetic Aperture Radar, Online, pp. 1–5 (2021)
12. Xing, S., Song, S., Quan, S., Sun, D., Wang, J., Li, Y.: Near-field 3D sparse SAR direct imaging with irregular samples. Remote Sens. (14), 246321 (2022). https://doi.org/10.3390/rs14246321
13. Liu, F., Huang, D., Cunqian Feng, C.: Translational motion compensation for maneuvering target echoes with sparse aperture based on dimension compressed optimization, Published 2022. IEEE Trans. Geosci. Remote Sens. Eng. (2022). https://doi.org/10.1109/TGRS.2022.3169275

14. Zhang, L., Wang, H., Qiao, Z.-J.: Resolution enhancement for ISAR imaging via improved statistical compressive sensing. EURASIP J. Adv. Sig. Process. **2016**, 80 (2016). https://doi.org/10.1186/s13634-016-0379-2

15. Zhang, L., Wang, H., Qiao, Z.-J.: Compensation of phase errors for compressed sensing based ISAR imagery using inadequate pulses. Progr. Electromagn. Res. M **41**, 125–138 (2015). https://doi.org/10.2528/PIERM14120402, http://www.jpier.org/PIERM/pier.php?paper=141 20402

16. Jiang, Y., Li, Y.: Algorithm-oriented SIMD computer mathematical model and its application. Int. J. Inf. Commun. Technol. Educ. Off. Publication Inf. Resourc. Manag. Assoc. IGI Global **18**(3), 1–18 (2022). https://doi.org/10.4018/IJICTE.315743

17. Ghaffari, A., Babaie-Zadeh, M., Jutten, C.: Sparse decomposition of two dimensional signals. In: ICASSP 2009 - IEEE International Conference on Acoustics, Speech and Signal Processing, April 2009, Taipei, Taiwan. pp. 3157–3160 (2009). ffhal-00400464f

18. Qiu, W., et al.: Compressive sensing–based algorithm for passive bistatic ISAR with DVB-T signals. IEEE Trans. Aerosp. Electron. Syst. **51**(3), 2166–2180 (2015). https://doi.org/10.1109/TAES.2015.130761

Probability Characteristics of CFAR Processors in Presence of Randomly Arriving Impulse Interference

Ivan Garvanov[⊠]

University of Library Studies and Information Technologies, Sofia, Bulgaria
i.garvanov@unibit.bg

Abstract. In the radar systems, the performance of signal detectors is seriously degraded by arrival of impulse noise that extremely worsens their detectability characteristics. In this paper, the randomly arriving impulse interference is mathematically described as Binominal pulse sequences. This model of impulse noise is used for numerical analysis of CA CFAR pulse detector and two types of CFAR pulse train detectors with binary (CFAR BI) and non-coherent (CFAR PI) integration. The detectability of detectors is expressed in terms of the detection probabilities and the Average Decision Threshold (ADT). The analytical expressions for calculating both quality characteristics, obtained in this paper, provide a basis for comparison analysis of CFAR detectors in the presence of Binomial and Poisson impulse noise. The detectability of typical pulse and pulse train detectors is numerical analyzed in the presence of Binomial and Poisson impulse noise. Therefore, the proposed detectors can be used in different radar systems

Keywords: radar signal processing · CFAR processor · randomly arriving impulse interference · average decision threshold · detection probability

1 Introduction

Conventional Cell-Averaging Constant False Alarm Rate (CA CFAR) detectors are very effective in case of stationary and homogeneous interference. In such noisy environment, the problem of target detection is formulated as detection of a single pulse on the background of Gaussian noise. In a CA CFAR detector, proposed by Finn and Johnson, pulse detection is declared if the signal value exceeds the threshold, which is formed by averaging the samples of the reference window surrounding the test cell [1]. The effectiveness of CA CFAR pulse detectors is very sensitive to non-stationary and non-homogeneous background and extremely degrades in the presence of strong randomly arriving impulse interference (impulse noise) in both, the test resolution cell and the reference window [2]. Such type of impulse noise can be caused by adjacent operating radar or other appliance generating "bursts" of interference. For example, the most well-known sources of impulse noise are the sparks, which occur in some electric devices, when any rapid change in current and voltage may radiate pulses of EM energy. As a result, the sparks may briefly produce far more power than the wanted signals at the

© The Author(s), under exclusive license to Springer Nature Switzerland AG 2023
B. Shishkov and A. Lazarov (Eds.): ICTRS 2023, CCIS 1990, pp. 17–32, 2023.
https://doi.org/10.1007/978-3-031-49263-1_2

receiver input. A particular problem with impulse noise is that it does not obey the same statistics as stationary noise. This combined with the high peak powers, means that it is a serious problem for CA CFAR detection, even if the received carrier power is well above the natural stationary background noise level.

In recent years different approaches have been proposed to improve the detectability of CFAR detectors operating in random impulse noise [2–18]. One of them is the use of ordered statistics for estimating the noise level in the reference window, proposed by Rohling [3]. In Ordered Statistic CFAR (OS CFAR) pulse detectors, the k'th ordered sample in the reference window is an estimate of the background level in the test resolution cell. The performance of such an OS CFAR detector in the presence of multipath interference in existing communication networks is evaluated and studied in [4]. Another approach to improve the performance of CFAR detectors in the presence of impulse interference is to excise high-power samples from the reference window before processing by a conventional CA CFAR pulse detector. This approach was used by Goldman for design of an excision CFAR detector (EXC CFAR) described in [5]. The similar method is used by Gandhi and Kassam, which suggested the structure of a Censored Mean Level (CML CFAR) detector, where the interference level estimate is found as a sum of the samples remained after removing of the lowest "k1" and the highest "k2" ordered samples from the reference window [2]. The performance of automatic CML CFAR detectors in non-homogeneous environment is proposed by Himonas and Barkat in [6]. The most important property of these detectors is their ability to determine and efficiently censor the unwanted samples in the reference window, which cause excessive false alarms. It must be noted that the CFAR detectors mentioned above are considered for the case of pulse detection.

The problem of detection of a pulse train in the presence of impulse noise is considered in [7, 8], where the performance of a conventional CA CFAR detector with binary integration (CA CFAR BI) is analyzed in impulse noise arriving with the relatively low average repetition frequency. Such a detector employs a two-step thresholding technique. In the first step a preliminary decision is made about each pulse of the pulse train reflected from the target. The pulse detection is carried out by a CA CFAR pulse detector and is declared if the sample in the range resolution cell under test exceeds the first adaptive threshold. The number of decisions where the first threshold is exceeded is counted and in the second step this number is compared with the second digital threshold. It is shown that the detectability of a conventional CA CFAR BI detector is drastically degraded in conditions of strong impulse interference when the interference-to-noise ratio (INR) is very large and the probability of occurrence of a random pulse in the reference window grows. To improve the detectability of such a detector in environment of impulse interference, the broadband transmission of linear frequency (LFM) or phase-code (PCM) modulated radar signals is proposed to be used in [9]. This technique is very effective in cases when the average impulse noise repetition interval exceeds the broadband pulse duration. In that case, even if the intensity of impulse interference is very strong, the detectability losses may be drastically decreased. The other technique that may be used to improve the detectability of a CA CFAR BI detector in the presence of impulse noise is to use a censoring technique proposed by Goldman before pulse detection and binary integration. Such an excision CFAR detector with binary integration (EXC CFAR BI) is proposed in [10], and its quality is analyzed for the case of Gaussian impulse noise. In this detector all strong samples that exceed the excision threshold are removed from the sample set prior to the cell-averaging procedure. The excision procedure ensures that the calculation of the pulse detection threshold is based on a set of samples purged of strong impulse noise and is, therefore, much more representative for noise level estimation. The analytical expressions for computing the detection probabilities obtained in [9, 10] enable to optimize a set of the most essential parameters of both, the CA CFAR BI detector and EXC CFAR BI detector, in the presence of Poisson impulse noise.

As noted above in [7–12], the quality of CA CFAR pulse train detectors is analyzed in the presence of impulse interference that arrival randomly in time from a single impulse-noise source. Such impulse interference can be mathematically described as a stochastic Poisson-model process, in which the occurrence of a random impulse in each range resolution cell is modeled as a Poisson event and the power of each random impulse is distributed according to the exponential law with a constant parameter. The other model of impulse noise is used for analysis of CFAR detectors in [13–18] where it is assumed that the impulse interference arrivals from two independent impulse-noise sources operating in parallel. Each of them generates a random impulse sequence with the same power intensity and the same average repetition frequency. In that case the impulse interference can be mathematically described as a stochastic Binomial-model process, in which the occurrence of a random impulse in each range resolution cell is modeled as a binomial event. The power of a random impulse generated by each impulse-noise source is distributed according to the exponential law with the same constant parameter.

The detectability of CFAR detectors can be evaluated in two possible ways. The first of them is to estimate the detectability losses in Signal-to-Noise Ratio (SNR) with respect to the situation of no impulse noise. These detectability losses are defined for given values of the probability of detection and false alarm. This conventional approach is used in [7–12] for evaluating the performance of CFAR pulse train detectors in the presence of Poisson impulse noise.

The other method for estimating the detectability of CFAR detectors is used in this paper. According to this method, the detectability of CFAR detectors is estimated in terms of the detectability losses in the ADT with respect to the situation of no impulse noise. The goal of this paper is to explore the detectability of two types of CFAR detectors in the presence of impulse noise by 1) evaluating the average decision threshold (ADT) of detectors (the usefulness of estimating the ADT for analysis of detectors was firstly demonstrated by Rohling in [3]) and 2) assuming that the impulse noise corresponds to the Binomial model.

Broadly speaking, this paper is an effort to summarize all our theoretical results in the analysis of CFAR pulse and pulse train detectors operating in the presence of Binomial impulse noise.

2 Signal Model

Let us assume that L pulses hit the target, which is modeled according to the Swerling case II. The received signal power is sampled in range by using $(N - 1)$ resolution cells resulting in a data matrix with $(N + 1)$ rows and L columns. Each row of the data matrix is of signal values obtained for L pulse repetition intervals in one range resolution cell. The sampling rate in range is such that the samples in each column are statistically independent. Let us also assume that the first "$N/2$" and the last "$N/2$" rows of the data matrix are used as reference cells to estimate the noise level in the test resolution cells of the data matrix. The test resolution cells are the "$N/2 + 1$" row of the data matrix. The distribution law of samples in the data matrix depends on the impulse noise model.

2.1 Binomial Impulse Noise

The Binomial model describes a situation when the impulse noise is derived from two independent and identical impulse-noise sources, each of which generates a random impulse sequence with the same power intensity and the same average repetition frequency [13–18]. The probability of occurrence (p) of a random pulse generated by each impulse-noise source in each range resolution cell can be expressed as $p = F.t$, where F is the average pulse repetition frequency of and t is the transmitted pulse duration. This means that the elements of the reference window are drawn from three classes. The first class represents the receiver noise only with probability $(1 - p)^2$. The second class represents a situation when the signal samples are corrupted by a random impulse generated by one or the other impulse-noise source. This situation occurs with probability $2p(1 - p)$. The third class represents a situation when the signal samples are corrupted by a total random pulse that is a sum of pulses generated by the two impulse-noise sources. This situation occurs with probability p^2. According to the theorem of total probability, the elements of the reference window are independent random variables distributed with the following probability density function (PDF):

$$f(x_i) = \frac{(1-p)^2}{\eta} exp\left(\frac{-x_i}{\eta}\right) + \frac{2p(1-p)}{\eta(1+I)} exp\left(\frac{-x_i}{\eta(1+I)}\right)$$

$$+ \frac{p^2}{\eta(1+2I)} exp\left(\frac{-x_i}{\eta(1+2I)}\right), i = 1, \ldots, N \qquad (1)$$

where η is the average power of the receiver noise, I is the average per pulse interference-to-noise ratio (INR) at the receiver input, and N is the number of samples in the reference window.

In the presence of a wanted signal in the test resolution cell the signal samples are independent random variables distributed with the following PDF:

$$f(x_{0l}) = \frac{(1-p)^2}{\eta(1+S)} exp\left(\frac{-x_{0l}}{\eta(1+S)}\right) + \frac{2p(1-p)}{\eta(1+I+S)} exp\left(\frac{-x_{0l}}{\eta(1+I+S)}\right)$$

$$+ \frac{p^2}{\eta(1+2I+S)} exp\left(\frac{-x_{0l}}{\eta(1+2I+S)}\right), l = 1, \ldots, L \qquad (2)$$

where S is the average per pulse signal-to-noise ratio (SNR).

2.2 Poisson Impulse Noise

The Poisson model describes a real radar situation when the impulse noise arrivals from a single impulse-noise source [7–12]. According to this model, in each range resolution cell the signal sample may be corrupted by impulse noise with constant probability p_0. Therefore, the elements of the reference window are drawn from two classes. One class represents the interference-plus-noise with probability p_0. The other class represents the receiver noise only with probability $(1 - p_0)$. According to the theorem of total probability, the elements of the reference window are independent random variables distributed with the following PDF:

$$f(x_i) = \frac{(1 - p_0)}{\eta} exp\left(\frac{-x_i}{\eta}\right) + \frac{p_0}{\eta(1 + I)} exp\left(\frac{-x_i}{\eta(1 + I)}\right) \tag{3}$$

In the presence of a desired signal in the test resolution cell the signal samples are independent random variables distributed with the following PDF:

$$f(x_{0l}) = \frac{(1 - p_0)}{\eta(1 + S)} exp\left(\frac{-x_{0l}}{\eta(1 + S)}\right) + \frac{p_0}{\eta(1 + I + S)} exp\left(\frac{-x_{0l}}{\eta(1 + I + S)}\right) \tag{4}$$

The probability of occurrence of a random pulse in each range resolution cell can be expressed as $p_0 = F.t$, where F is the average pulse repetition frequency of and t is the transmitted pulse duration. It must be noted that if the probability p_0 is small $p_0 < 0.1$, the size of a reference window N is large, and $Np_0 = const$, then the model may be approximated with a Poisson model of impulse noise.

3 Analysis of CFAR Pulse Detector

In a conventional CFAR pulse detector the estimate of the noise level V is calculated by using the samples of the reference window $\{x_i\}_N$ surrounding the test cell. The threshold of pulse detection H_D is a product of the estimate V and the predetermined detection scale factor T, i.e., $H_D = VT$. The pulse detection is declared, if the sample x_0 from the test resolution cell exceeds the threshold H_D:

$$\begin{cases} H_0 : x_0 < H_D \\ H_1 : x_0 \geq H_D \end{cases} \tag{5}$$

where H_1 is the hypothesis that the test resolution cell contains a desired signal and H_0 is the hypothesis that the test resolution cell contains the receiver noise only.

According to the decision rule (5), the probability of pulse detection P_D and false alarm P_{FA} are defined as

$$P_D = \int_0^\infty f_v(V)dV \int_{H_D}^\infty f(x_0/H_1)dx_0 \tag{6}$$

$$P_{FA} = \int_0^\infty f_v(V)dV \int_{H_D}^\infty f(x_0/H_0)dx_0 \tag{7}$$

where $f_v(V)$ is the PDF of the estimate V, $f(x_0/H_1)$ is the conditional PDF of the test sample under hypothesis H_1, and $f(x_0/H_0)$ is the conditional PDF of the test sample under hypothesis H_0. The detection scale factor T is determined to maintain a required probability of false alarm P_{FA}.

According to [3], the average decision threshold (ADT) of a CFAR pulse detector is defined as a normalized value:

$$ADT_{CFAR} = \frac{E(VT)}{\eta} \tag{8}$$

where E is the mathematical expectation of V calculated as:

$$\frac{E(V)}{\eta} = -\frac{d}{dT} M_V\left(\frac{T}{\eta}\right)\Big|_{T=0} \tag{9}$$

Mostly, the efficiency of detection is evaluated in terms of the detectability losses in SNR with respect to the situation of no impulse noise. The detectability losses are defined for given values of the probabilities of detection and false alarm.

In this paper, the detectability of pulse detectors is estimated by the detectability losses in ADT according to [3]. In that case, the detectability losses (Δ) are defined as the ratio of the two ADTs defined for given values of the probability of detection and false alarm. These losses are calculated as:

$$\Delta[dB] = 10lg\left[\frac{ADT_1}{ADT_2}\right] = 10lg\left[\frac{E(V_1T_1)}{E(V_2T_2)}\right] \tag{10}$$

For $P_{FA1} = P_{FA2}$, $P_{D1} = P_{D2} = 0.5$, where P_{FA1} and P_{D1} are the probabilities of detection and false alarm calculated for the case when the impulse noise is present at the receiver input, and P_{FA2} and P_{D2} are the probabilities of detection calculated for the case of no impulse noise.

In a conventional CA CFAR pulse detector proposed by Finn and Johnson, the noise level is estimated by averaging the outputs of the reference cells surrounding the test cell [1].

$$V = \sum_{i=1}^{N} x_i \tag{11}$$

3.1 CA CFAR Detector in Binomial Impulse Noise

For a conventional CA CFAR pulse detector, where the noise level is estimated by (11), the probability of pulse detection is readily computed using the expressions (2) and (6):

$$P_D = (1 - p)^2 M_V\left(\frac{T}{\eta(1 + S)}\right) + 2p(1 - p)M_V\left(\frac{T}{\eta(1 + I + S)}\right)$$
$$+ p^2 M_V\left(\frac{T}{\eta(1 + 2I + S)}\right) \tag{12}$$

where $M_V(.)$ is the moment generating function (MGF) of the noise level estimate V.

According to (12), the MGF of the noise level estimate V is calculated as a product of the MGF of all samples in the reference window, i.e., $M_V(U) = M_x^N(U)$, where $M_x(U)$ is the MGF of the random variable x_i and defined as:

$$M_x(U) = \int_0^\infty exp(-Ux)f(x)dx \qquad (13)$$

In case of Binomial impulse noise, the PDF of each sample in the reference window, $f(x)$, is defined by (1), and therefore the corresponding MGF is:

$$M_x(U) = \frac{(1-p)^2}{1+U\eta} + \frac{2p(1-p)}{1+U\eta(1+I)} + \frac{p^2}{1+U\eta(1+2I)} \qquad (14)$$

Using (14), the MGF of the estimate V is calculated.

$$M_V(U) = \sum_{i=0}^{N} \frac{C_N^i p^{2i}}{1+U\eta(1+2I)} \sum_{j=0}^{N-i} \frac{C_{N-i}^j(2p(1-p))^j}{(1+U\eta(1+I))^j} \frac{(1-p)^{2(N-i-j)}}{(1+U\eta)^{N-i-j}} \qquad (15)$$

Replacing $M_V(U)$ in (12) by (15), the analytical expression for calculating the probability of pulse detection takes the form [13].

$$P_D = \sum_{i=0}^{N} C_N^i p^{2i} \sum_{i=0}^{N-1} C_{N-i}^j(2p(1-p))^j(1-p)^{2(N-i-j)}\{R_1 + R_2 + R_3\} \qquad (16)$$

$$R_1 = \frac{(1-p)^2}{\left(1+\frac{T(1+2I)}{1+S}\right)^i\left(1+\frac{T(1+I)}{1+S}\right)^j\left(1+\frac{T}{1+S}\right)^{N-i-j}}$$

$$R_2 = \frac{2p(1-p)}{\left(1+\frac{T(1+2I)}{1+I+S}\right)^i\left(1+\frac{T(1+I)}{1+I+S}\right)^j\left(1+\frac{T}{1+I+S}\right)^{N-i-j}}$$

$$R_3 = \frac{p^2}{\left(1+\frac{T(1+2I)}{1+2I+S}\right)^i\left(1+\frac{T(1+I)}{1+2I+S}\right)^j\left(1+\frac{T}{1+2I+S}\right)^{N-i-j}}$$

The probability of false alarm is evaluated by (16), where $S = 0$.

3.2 CA CFAR Detector in Poisson Impulse Noise

In case of Poisson impulse noise, the analytical expression for calculating the probability of pulse detection is obtained in [7].

$$P_{0D} = \sum_{i=0}^{N} C_N^i p_0^i(1-p_0)^{(N-i)}\{R_{01} + R_{02}\} \qquad (17)$$

$$R_{01} = \frac{p_0}{\left(1+\frac{T(1+I)}{1+I+S}\right)^i\left(1+\frac{T}{1+I+S}\right)^{N-i}}$$

$$R_{02} = \frac{1-p_0}{\left(1 + \frac{T(1+I)}{1+S}\right)^i \left(1 + \frac{T}{1+S}\right)^{N-i}}$$

It can be easy seen that the same expression can be obtained from (16) under the assumption that $p^2 \to 0$, $2p(1-p) \to p_0$ and $(1-p)^2 \to (1-p_0)$. It is the case when the probability of co-occurrence of the two random pulses in each range resolution cell becomes negligible, i.e. p^2 tends to 0, but the probability of occurrence of a random pulse derived from one of two impulse-noise sources is non-zero, i.e. $2p(1-p) > 0$. The probability of false alarm is calculated by (17), setting $S = 0$.

3.3 Average Decision Threshold of CA CFAR Detectors

In case of Binomial impulse noise, the average decision threshold (ADT) of a CA CFAR pulse detector is calculated by using Eqs. (9, 15). After substituting $U = \frac{T}{\eta}$ into (15), differentiating it with respect to T and substituting $T = 0$, the expression for calculating the ADT takes the form: [13]

$$ADT = T \sum_{i=0}^{N} C_N^i p^{2i} \sum_{j=0}^{N-i} C_{N-i}^j (2p(1-p))^j (1-p)^{2(N-i-j)} (N + I(2i+j)) \quad (18)$$

where the detection scale factor T is found as a solution of the Eq. (16), for a required value of the probability of false alarm P_{FA} and $S = 0$.

In case of Poisson impulse noise, the expression for calculating the ADT can be easily obtained from (17) assuming that $p^2 \to 0$, $2p(1-p) \to p_0$ and $(1-p)^2 \to (1-p_0)$ [16]:

$$ADT = T \sum_{i=0}^{N} C_N^i p_0^i (1-p_0)^{(N-i)} (N + iI) \quad (19)$$

where the detection scale factor T is found as a solution of the Eq. (17), for a required value of the probability of false alarm P_{FA} and $S = 0$.

For comparison, in case of no impulse noise, the expression for calculating the ADT is obtained in [2]:

$$ADT = TN, \text{ where } T = (P_{FA})^{-\frac{1}{N}} - 1 \quad (20)$$

4 Analysis of CFAR Pulse Train Detectors

4.1 Analysis of CFAR Detectors with Binary Integration

In a conventional CFAR pulse train detector with binary integration, the binary integrator counts L decisions (Φ_l) at the output of a CFAR pulse detector. The pulse train detection is declared if this sum exceeds the second digital threshold M. The decision rule is:

$$\begin{cases} H_1 : if \ \sum_{l=1}^{L} \Phi_l \geq M \\ H_0 : \quad otherwise \end{cases} \quad (21)$$

where L is the number of pulse transmissions, $\Phi_l = 0$ if no pulse is detected, and $\Phi_l = 1$ if pulse detection is indicated. The probability of pulse train detection is evaluated by:

$$P_{DBI} = \sum_{l=M}^{L} C_L^l P_D^l (1 - P_D)^{L-l} \tag{22}$$

where P_D is the probability of pulse detection, which may be found using the expressions (16) – for Binomial impulse noise and the expressions (17) – for Poisson impulse noise. The probability of false alarm is evaluated by (22), setting $S = 0$.

4.2   Analysis of CFAR Detectors with Non-coherent Integration

In a CFAR pulse train detector with non-coherent integration (CFAR PI), the noise level estimate is calculated by averaging the samples from the two-dimensional reference window [11, 12].

$$V = \sum_{l=1}^{L} \sum_{n=1}^{N} x_{ln} \tag{23}$$

Let q_o be a non-coherent sum of the elements from the test resolution cell.

$$q_0 = \sum_{l=1}^{L} x_{0l} \tag{24}$$

The pulse train is detected using the following decision rule:

$$\begin{cases} H_1 : & if \ q_0 \geq T_{PI} V \\ H_0 : & otherwise \end{cases} \tag{25}$$

where H_1 is the hypothesis that the test resolution cell contains the echoes from the target, and H_0 is the alternative. The probability of pulse train detection is determined as [12]

$$P_D = P(q_0 > T_{PI} V / H_1) = \int_0^{\infty} f_v(V) dV \int_{T_{PI} V}^{\infty} f_{q_0}(q_0 / H_1) dq_0 \tag{26}$$

where $f_V(V)$ is the PDF of the noise level estimate V and $f_{q_0}(q_0/H_1)$ is the conditional PDF of the test integrated signal q_0 under hypothesis H_1. The probability of false alarm is determined by:

$$P_{FA} = P(q_0 < T_{PI} V / H_0) = \int_0^{\infty} f_v(V) dV \int_{T_{PI} V}^{\infty} f_{q_0}(q_0 / H_0) dq_0 \tag{27}$$

where $f_{q_0}(q_0/H_0)$ is the conditional PDF of the integrated signal sample q_0 under hypothesis H_0. The scale factor T_{PI} is evaluated as a solution of the Eq. (27) to maintain a required value of the probability of false alarm.

4.2.1 CFAR PI Detector in Binominal Impulse Noise

In a CFAR PI pulse train detector, the two-dimensional window of size (LN) is used for calculation of the noise level estimate V. It is assumed that the noise level estimate V is a sum of (LN) independent and identically distributed random variables with the PDF defined by (1). Using (15), the MGF of the estimate V can be expressed as follows:

$$M_V(U) = \sum_{i=0}^{LN} C_{LN}^i p^{2i} \sum_{j=0}^{LN-i} \frac{C_{LN-i}^j (2p(1-p))^j}{(1+U\eta^*)^j(1+U\eta^{2*})^i} \frac{(1-p)^{2(N-i-j)}}{(1+U\eta)^{LN-i-j}} \quad (28)$$

where $\eta^* = \eta^*(1+I)$ and $\eta^{2*} = \eta^*(1+2I)$.

The PDF of the estimate V can be found as the inverse Laplacian transformation of its MGF, that is $f_V(V) = Laplace^{-1}\{M_V(U)\}$.

Denoting the linear operator of summation in (28) as:

$$A = \sum_{i=0}^{LN} C_{LN}^i p^{2i} \sum_{j=0}^{LN-i} C_{LN-i}^j (2p(1-p))^j (1-p)^{2(N-i-j)} \quad (29)$$

we can write the expression for the PDF of the estimate V:

$$f_V(V) = A\left\{ \frac{1}{(j-1)!} lim_{U\to\left(\frac{-1}{\eta^*}\right)} \left[\frac{exp(UV)}{(\eta^*)^j(1+U\eta^{2*})^i(1+U\eta)^{LN-i-j}} \right]^{(j-1)} \right. \quad (30)$$

$$+ \frac{1}{(i-1)!} lim_{U\to\left(\frac{-1}{\eta^{2*}}\right)} \left[\frac{exp(UV)}{(\eta^{2*})^i(1+U\eta^*)^j(1+U\eta)^{LN-i-j}} \right]^{(i-1)}$$

$$+ \left. \frac{1}{(LN-i-j-1)!} lim_{U\to\left(\frac{-1}{\eta}\right)} \left[\frac{exp(UV)}{(\eta)^{LN-i-j}(1+U\eta^*)^j(1+U\eta^{2*})^i} \right]^{(LN-i-j-1)} \right\}$$

The expression (31) can be rewritten in a simple form as:

$$f_V(V) = A\{f_1(V) + f_2(V) + f_3(V)\} \quad (31)$$

where the functions $f_1(V), f_2(V)$ and $f_3(V)$ are calculated as:

$$f_1(V) = \sum_{a=0}^{j-1} \frac{V^a exp(-V/\eta^*)}{a!(\eta^*)^{a+1}} Q_1, \quad (32)$$

$$f_2(V) = \sum_{a=0}^{i-1} \frac{V^a exp(-V/\eta^{2*})}{a!(\eta^{2*})^{a+1}} Q_2$$

$$f_2(V) = \sum_{a=0}^{LN-i-j-1} \frac{V^a exp(-V/\eta)}{a!(\eta)^{a+1}} Q_3$$

The coefficients Q_1, Q_2, and Q_3 in (32) are calculated as

$$Q_1 = (-1)^{LN-j} \sum_{b=0}^{j-1-a} \binom{i-1-b}{b} \binom{LN-i-a-b-2}{LN-i-j-1}. \quad (33)$$

$$\cdot \left(\frac{\eta^{2*}}{\eta^{2*} - \eta^*} \right)^{i+b} \left(\frac{\eta}{\eta - \eta^*} \right)^{LN-i-a-b-1} \left(\frac{\eta^*}{\eta^{2*}} \right)^{i} \left(\frac{\eta^*}{\eta} \right)^{LN-i-j}$$

$$Q_2 = (-1)^{LN-j} \sum_{b=0}^{i-1-a} \binom{i-1-b}{b} \binom{LN-j-a-b-2}{LN-i-j-1}.$$

$$\cdot \left(\frac{\eta^*}{\eta^* - \eta^{2*}} \right)^{j+b} \left(\frac{\eta}{\eta - \eta^{2*}} \right)^{LN-j-a-b-1} \left(\frac{\eta^{2*}}{\eta^*} \right)^{j} \left(\frac{\eta^{2*}}{\eta} \right)^{LN-i-j}$$

$$Q_3 = (-1)^{i+j} \sum_{b=0}^{LN-i-j-1-a} \binom{j-1+b}{b} \binom{LN-j-a-b-2}{i-1}.$$

$$\cdot \left(\frac{\eta^*}{\eta^* - \eta} \right)^{j+b} \left(\frac{\eta^{2*}}{\eta^{2*} - \eta} \right)^{LN-j-a-b-1} \left(\frac{\eta}{\eta^{2*}} \right)^{i} \left(\frac{\eta}{\eta^*} \right)^{j}$$

Using (15), the MGF of q_0, which is a sum of the samples from the test resolution cells, is expressed as:

$$M_{q_0}(U) = \sum_{n=0}^{L} C_L^n p^{2n} \sum_{m=0}^{L-n} \frac{C_{L-n}^m (2p(1-p))^m}{(1+U\eta_s^*)^m (1+U\eta_s^{2*})^n} \frac{(1-p)^{2(L-n-m)}}{(1+U\eta_s)^{L-n-m}} \qquad (34)$$

where $\eta_s = \eta(1+S)$, $\eta_s^* = \eta(1+S+I)$ and $\eta_s^{2*} = \eta(1+S+2I)$.

The PDF of the random variable q_0 can be found as the inverse Laplacian transformation of its MGF, that is $f_{q_0}(V) = Laplace^{-1}\{M_{q_0}(U)\}$.

Denoting the operator of summation in (34) as:

$$B = \sum_{n=0}^{L} C_L^n p^{2n} \sum_{m=0}^{L-n} C_{L-n}^m (2p(1-p))^m (1-p)^{2(L-n-m)} \qquad (35)$$

we can write the expression for the MGF of the random variable q_0 as:

$$f_{q_0}\left(\frac{q_0}{H_1} \right) = B \left\{ \frac{1}{(m-1)!} \lim_{q_0 \to \left(\frac{-1}{\eta^*} \right)} \left[\frac{exp(Uq_0)}{(\eta_s^*)^m (1+U\eta_s^{2*})^n (1+U\eta_s)^{L-n-m}} \right]^{(m-1)} \right.$$

$$\qquad (36)$$

$$+ \frac{1}{(n-1)!} \lim_{q_0 \to \left(\frac{-1}{\eta^{2*}} \right)} \left[\frac{exp(Uq_0)}{(\eta_s^{2*})^n (1+U\eta_s^*)^m (1+U\eta_s)^{L-n-m}} \right]^{(n-1)}$$

$$+ \frac{1}{(L-n-m-1)!} \lim_{q_0 \to \left(\frac{-1}{\eta} \right)} \left[\frac{exp(Uq_0)}{(\eta_s)^{L-n-m} (1+U\eta_s^*)^m (1+U\eta_s^{2*})^n} \right]^{(L-n-m-1)} \right\}$$

The expression (34) can be rewritten in a simple form as:

$$f_{q_0}(q_0/H_1) = B\{f_1(q_0) + f_2(q_0) + f_3(q_0)\} \qquad (37)$$

where the functions $f_1(q_0), f_2(q_0)$ and $f_3(q_0)$ are calculated as:

$$f_1(q_0) = \sum_{c=0}^{m-1} \frac{q_0^c exp\left(-q_0/\eta_s^*\right)}{c!\left(\eta_s^*\right)^{c+1}} Q_1^s \tag{38}$$

$$f_2(q_0) = \sum_{c=0}^{n-1} \frac{q_0^c exp\left(-q_0/\eta_s^{2*}\right)}{c!\left(\eta_s^{2*}\right)^{c+1}} Q_2^s,$$

$$f_2(q_0) = \sum_{v=0}^{L-n-m-1} \frac{q_0^c exp(-q_0/\eta_s)}{c!(\eta_s)^{c+1}} Q_3^s.$$

The coefficients Q_1^s, Q_2^s, and Q_3^s in (38) are calculated as:

$$Q_1^s = (-1)^{L-m} \sum_{d=0}^{m-1-c} \binom{n-1+d}{d}\binom{L-n-c-d-2}{L-n-m-1}. \tag{39}$$

$$\cdot \left(\frac{\eta_s^{2*}}{\eta_s^{2*}-\eta_s^*}\right)^{n+d} \left(\frac{\eta_s}{\eta_s-\eta_s^*}\right)^{L-n-c-d-1} \left(\frac{\eta_s^*}{\eta_s^{2*}}\right)^n \left(\frac{\eta_s^*}{\eta_s}\right)^{L-n-m}$$

$$Q_2^s = (-1)^{L-n} \sum_{d=0}^{n-1-c} \binom{m-1+d}{d}\binom{L-m-c-d-2}{L-n-m-1}.$$

$$\cdot \left(\frac{\eta_s^*}{\eta_s^*-\eta_s^{2*}}\right)^{m+d} \left(\frac{\eta_s}{\eta_s-\eta_s^{2*}}\right)^{L-m-c-d-1} \left(\frac{\eta_s^{2*}}{\eta_s^*}\right)^m \left(\frac{\eta_s^{2*}}{\eta_s}\right)^{L-n-m}$$

$$Q_3^s = (-1)^{n+m} \sum_{d=0}^{L-n-m-1-c} \binom{m-1+d}{d}\binom{L-m-c-d-2}{n-1}.$$

$$\cdot \left(\frac{\eta_s^*}{\eta_s^*-\eta_s}\right)^{m+d} \left(\frac{\eta_s^{2*}}{\eta_s^{2*}-\eta_s}\right)^{L-m-c-d-1} \left(\frac{\eta_s}{\eta_s^{2*}}\right)^n \left(\frac{\eta_s}{\eta_s^*}\right)^m$$

The probability of pulse train detection P_D is calculated by (26), replacing the corresponding PDF by its expressions (31) and (37).

$$P_D = AB \int_0^\infty [f_1(V) + f_2(V) + f_3(V)]dV. \tag{40}$$

$$\cdot \left[\int_{VT_{PI}}^\infty f_1(q_0)dq_0 + \int_{VT_{PI}}^\infty f_2(q_0)dq_0 + \int_{VT_{PI}}^\infty f_3(q_0)dq_0 \right] =$$

$$= AB \int_0^\infty [f_1(V) + f_2(V) + f_3(V)][I_1(V) + I_2(V) + I_3(V)]dV$$

where the functions $I_1(V)$, $I_2(V)$, and $I_3(V)$ may be presented as:

$$I_1(V) = \sum_{c=0}^{m-1} Q_1^s \sum_{l=0}^{c} \left(\frac{VT_{PI}}{\eta_s^*}\right)^l \frac{exp(-VT_{PI}/\eta_s^*)}{l!}, \tag{41}$$

$$I_2(V) = \sum_{c=0}^{n-1} Q_2^s \sum_{l=0}^{c} \left(\frac{VT_{PI}}{\eta_s^{2*}}\right)^l \frac{exp(-VT_{PI}/\eta_s^{2*})}{l!},$$

$$I_3(V) = \sum_{c=0}^{L-n-m-1} Q_3^s \sum_{l=0}^{c} \left(\frac{VT_{PI}}{\eta_s}\right)^l \frac{exp(-VT_{PI}/\eta_s)}{l!}.$$

Finally, the expression for calculating the probability of pulse train detection can be rewritten as:

$$P_{DPI} = AB(F_1 + F_2 + F_3 + \ldots + F_9) \tag{42}$$

where the quantities $F_i (i = 1..9)$ enters in the expression (42) with the expressions:

$$F_1 = \sum_{c=0}^{m-1} Q_1^s \sum_{l=0}^{c} \left(\frac{\eta_s^* T_{PI}}{\eta_s^* + \eta_s^* T_{PI}}\right)^l \sum_{a=0}^{l} Q_1\binom{a+l}{l}\left(\frac{\eta_s^*}{\eta_s^* + \eta_s^* T_{PI}}\right)^{a+1} \tag{43}$$

$$F_2 = \sum_{c=0}^{n-1} Q_2^s \sum_{l=0}^{c} \left(\frac{\eta_s^* T_{PI}}{\eta_s^{2*} + \eta_s^* T_{PI}}\right)^l \sum_{a=0}^{l} Q_1\binom{a+l}{l}\left(\frac{\eta_s^{2*}}{\eta_s^{2*} + \eta_s^* T_{PI}}\right)^{a+1}$$

$$F_3 = \sum_{c=0}^{L-n-m-1} Q_3^g \sum_{l=0}^{c} \left(\frac{\eta_s^* T_{PI}}{\eta_s + \eta_s^* T_{PI}}\right)^l \sum_{a=0}^{l} Q_1\binom{a+l}{l}\left(\frac{\eta_s}{\eta_s + \eta_s^* T_{PI}}\right)^{a+1}$$

$$F_4 = \sum_{c=0}^{m-1} Q_1^s \sum_{l=0}^{c} \left(\frac{\eta_s^{2*} T_{PI}}{\eta_s^* + \eta_s^{2*} T_{PI}}\right)^l \sum_{a=0}^{l} Q_2\binom{a+l}{l}\left(\frac{\eta_s^*}{\eta_s^* + \eta_s^{2*} T_{PI}}\right)^{a+1}$$

$$F_5 = \sum_{c=0}^{n-1} Q_2^s \sum_{l=0}^{c} \left(\frac{\eta_s^{2*} T_{PI}}{\eta_s^{2*} + \eta_s^{2*} T_{PI}}\right)^l \sum_{a=0}^{l} Q_2\binom{a+l}{l}\left(\frac{\eta_s^{2*}}{\eta_s^{2*} + \eta_s^{2*} T_{PI}}\right)^{a+1}$$

$$F_6 = \sum_{c=0}^{L-n-m-1} Q_3^s \sum_{l=0}^{c} \left(\frac{\eta_s^{2*} T_{PI}}{\eta_s + \eta_s^{2*} T_{PI}}\right)^l \sum_{a=0}^{l} Q_2\binom{a+l}{l}\left(\frac{\eta_s}{\eta_s + \eta_s^{2*} T_{PI}}\right)^{a+1}$$

$$F_7 = \sum_{c=0}^{m-1} Q_1^s \sum_{l=0}^{c} \left(\frac{\eta_s T_{PI}}{\eta_s^* + \eta_s T_{PI}}\right)^l \sum_{a=0}^{LN-i-j-1} Q_3\binom{a+l}{l}\left(\frac{\eta_s^*}{\eta_s^* + \eta_s T_{PI}}\right)^{a+1}$$

$$F_8 = \sum_{c=0}^{n-1} Q_2^s \sum_{l=0}^{c} \left(\frac{\eta_s T_{PI}}{\eta_s^{2*} + \eta_s T_{PI}}\right)^l \sum_{a=0}^{LN-i-j-1} Q_3\binom{a+l}{l}\left(\frac{\eta_s^{2*}}{\eta_s^{2*} + \eta_s T_{PI}}\right)^{a+1}$$

$$F_9 = \sum_{c=0}^{L-n-m-1} Q_3^s \sum_{l=0}^{c} \left(\frac{\eta T_{PI}}{\eta_s + \eta T_{PI}}\right)^l \sum_{a=0}^{LN-i-j-1} Q_3\binom{a+l}{l}\left(\frac{\eta_s}{\eta_s + \eta T_{PI}}\right)^{a+1}$$

The probability of false alarm is calculated by setting $S = 0$ into the expression (40).

4.2.2   CFAR PI Detector in Poisson Impulse Noise

In case of Poisson impulse noise, the expression for calculating the probability of pulse detection is obtained in [12].

$$P_D = \sum_{i=1}^{LN} C_{LN}^i p^i (1-p)^{LN-i} \sum_{j=1}^{L} C_{L}^j p^j (1-p)^{L-j} (F_1 + F_2 + F_3 + F_4) \qquad (44)$$

where the functions F_1, F_2, F_3 and F_4 are calculated as

$$F_1 = \sum_{n=0}^{L-j-1} c_{n,j} \sum_{l=0}^{n} \left(\frac{\eta T_{PI}}{\eta_s + \eta T_{PI}}\right)^l \sum_{k=0}^{LN-i-1} \binom{k+l}{l} \left(\frac{\eta_s}{\eta_s + \eta T_{PI}}\right)^{k+1} a_{k,i} \qquad (45)$$

$$F_2 = \sum_{n=0}^{j-1} d_{n,j} \sum_{l=0}^{n} \left(\frac{\eta T_{PI}}{\eta_s^* + \eta T_{PI}}\right)^l \sum_{k=0}^{LN-i-1} \binom{k+l}{l} \left(\frac{\eta_s^*}{\eta_s^* + \eta T_{PI}}\right)^{k+1} a_{k,i}$$

$$F_3 = \sum_{n=0}^{L-j-1} c_{n,j} \sum_{l=0}^{n} \left(\frac{\eta_s^* T_{PI}}{\eta_s + \eta_s^* T_{PI}}\right)^l \sum_{k=0}^{i-1} \binom{k+l}{l} \left(\frac{\eta_s}{\eta_s + \eta_s^* T_{PI}}\right)^{k+1} b_{k,i}$$

$$F_4 = \sum_{n=0}^{j-1} d_{n,j} \sum_{l=0}^{n} \left(\frac{\eta^* T_{PI}}{\eta_s^* + \eta^* T_{PI}}\right)^l \sum_{k=0}^{i-1} \binom{k+l}{l} \left(\frac{\eta_s^*}{\eta_s^* + \eta^* T_{PI}}\right)^{k+1} b_{k,i}$$

$$a_{k,i} = (-1)^i \left(\frac{\eta}{\eta^*}\right)^i \binom{LN-k-2}{i-1} \left(\frac{\eta^*}{\eta^* - \eta}\right)^{LN-k-1}$$

$$b_{k,i} = (-1)^{LN-i} \left(\frac{\eta^*}{\eta}\right)^{LN-i} \binom{LN-k-2}{LN-i-1} \left(\frac{\eta}{\eta - \eta^*}\right)^{LN-k-1}$$

$$c_{n,j} = (-1)^j \left(\frac{\eta_s}{\eta_s^*}\right)^j \binom{L-n-2}{L-j-1} \left(\frac{\eta_s^*}{\eta_s^* - \eta_s}\right)^{L-n-1}$$

$$d_{n,j} = (-1)^{L-j} \left(\frac{\eta_s^*}{\eta_s}\right)^{L-j} \binom{L-n-2}{L-j-1} \left(\frac{\eta_s^* \eta_s}{\eta_s - \eta_s^*}\right)^{L-n-1}$$

It can be easy seen that the same expressions can be obtained from (42) under the assumptions that $p^2 \to 0$, $2p(1-p) \to p_0$ and $(1-p)^2 \to (1-p_0)$. It is the case when the probability of co-occurrence of two random pulses in each range resolution cell becomes negligible, i.e. p^2 tends to 0, but the probability of occurrence of a random pulse from one of two impulse-noise sources is non-zero, i.e. $2p(1-p) > 0$.

The probability of false alarm is calculated by (44), setting $S = 0$.

The expression (40) may be used for analysis of different types of detectors with non-coherent integration, discussed in the radar literature, for different models of radar environment.

5   Conclusions

In this paper, two models of impulse noise (Binomial and Poisson) are used for mathematical description of impulse noise at the receiver input. The Binomial model describes a radar situation when the impulse noise is derived from two independent and identical impulse-noise sources, each of which generates random pulses with the same power intensity and the same average repetition frequency. The Poisson model describes a simpler radar situation when the impulse noise is created by a single impulse-noise source. The detectability of detectors is expressed in terms of the detectability losses in the ADT calculated for given values of the probabilities of detection and false alarm.

For comparison, the analytical expressions for calculating the quality characteristics of detectors are presented not only for the Binomial model, but for the Poisson model as well. It is shown that the expressions for the Poisson model can be easily obtained from the corresponding expressions for the Binomial model.

Acknowledgement. This work was supported by the National Science Program "Security and Defense", which has received funding from the Ministry of Education and Science of the Republic of Bulgaria under the grant agreement № D01-74 /19.05.2022.

References

1. Finn, H.M., Johnson, R.S.: Adaptive detection mode with threshold control as a function of spatially sampled clutter estimation. RCA Rev. **29**(3), 414–464 (1968)
2. Gandhi, P., Kassam, S.: Analysis of CFAR processors in non-homogeneous background. IEEE Trans. **AES-24**(4), 443–454 (1988)
3. Rohling, H.: Radar CFAR thresholding in clutter and multiple target situations. IEEE Trans. **AES-19**(4), 608–621 (1983)
4. Kabakchiev, Chr., Kyovtorov, V., Garvanov, I.: OS CFAR detector for PN signal processing in multipath interference. In: Proceedings of of IEEE - International Radar Conference "Radar 2004", Toulouse, France, CD - 6P-SP-121, 6 p. (2004)
5. Goldman, H.: Performance of the excision CFAR detector in the presence of interferers. IEE Proc. **137**(3), 163–171 (1990)
6. Himonas, S., Barkat, M.: Automatic censored CFAR detection for non-homogeneous environments. IEEE Trans. **AES-28**(1), 286–304 (1992)
7. Behar, V.: CA CFAR radar signal detection in pulse jamming. Comptes Rendus de l'Academie Bulgare des Sci. **49**(12), 57–60 (1996)
8. Kabakchiev, Ch., Behar, V.: CFAR radar image detection in pulse jamming. In: IEEE Fourth International Symposium on ISSSTA'96, Mainz, Germany, pp. 182–185 (1996)
9. Kabakchiev, Ch., Behar, V.: Techniques for CFAR radar image detection in pulse jamming. In: 26-th European Microwave Conference on EuMC'96, Prague, Czech Republic, pp. 347–352 (1996)
10. Behar, V., Kabakchiev, Chr.: Excision CFAR binary integration processors. Comptes Rendus de l'Academie Bulgare des Sci. **49**(11/12), 61–64 (1996)
11. Himonas, S.: CFAR integration processors in randomly arriving impulse interference. IEEE Trans. **AES-30**(3), 809–816 (1994)
12. Behar, V., Kabakchiev, C., Dukovska, L.: Adaptive CFAR processor for radar target detection in pulse jamming. J. VLSI Sig. Proc. **26**(3), 383–396 (2000)

13. Garvanov, I.: CFAR BI detector in binomial distribution pulse jamming. Comptes Rendus de l'Academie Bulgare des Sciences **56**(10), 37–44 (2003)
14. Garvanov, I., Kabakchiev, Chr.: Excision CFAR BI detector in randomly arriving impulse interference. In: Proceedings of IEEE International Radar Conference on RADAR'2005, Arlington, USA, pp. 950–955, May 2005
15. Garvanov, I.: CFAR PI detector in the presence of binomial distribution flow from randomly arriving impulse interference. Comptes Rendus de l'Academie Bulgare des Sci. **58**(5), 545–552 (2005)
16. Garvanov, I., Kabakchiev, C.: Average decision threshold of CA CFAR and excision CFAR detectors in the presence of strong pulse jamming. In: Proceedings of GRS' 2002, pp. 615–620 (2002)
17. Garvanov, I., Kabakchiev, Chr.: Sensitivity of CFAR processors toward the change of input distribution of pulse jamming. In: Proceedings of IEEE International Conference on Radar' 2003, Adelaide, Australia, pp. 121–126 (2003)
18. Garvanov, I., Behar, V., Kabakchiev, C.: CFAR processors in pulse jamming. In: Dimov, I., Lirkov, I., Margenov, S., Zlatev, Z. (eds.) NMA 2002. LNCS, vol. 2542, pp. 291–298. Springer, Heidelberg (2003). https://doi.org/10.1007/3-540-36487-0_32

Influence of Advance Time on Accuracy of the Ionospheric Total Electron Content Forecast

Olga A. Maltseva[✉] and Artem M. Kharakhashyan

Institute for Physics, Southern Federal University, Rostov-on-Don 344090, Russia
oamaltseva@sfedu.ru

Abstract. The total electron content of the ionosphere plays an important role in determining the operational conditions for various technological systems, therefore, great importance is attached to its study and forecasting. In connection with the revival of the intensive use of machine learning methods, in the first work of the authors, using the example of the reference station Juliusruh and 2015, the effectiveness of traditional models of Long Short-Term Memory (LSTM) and Gated Recurrent Unit (GRU) was studied. In this paper, in order to increase the accuracy of the forecast, several modifications of these methods were proposed: 1) implementing the proposed MidR and InR architectures based on LSTM and GRU, 2) modifying the architectures using bidirectional algorithms, 3) using the temporal convolution architecture separately and jointly with bidirectional networks, thus, defining 10 architectures under study. In addition to the previous results for an advance time of 2h, the forecast was made for the traditionally used period of 24h. It is shown that four architectures of the first group and separately TCN provide prediction accuracy at the level of literature data, and for prediction for 24h, the prediction accuracy is 2 times worse than for 2h. The inclusion of the bidirectional algorithm leads to a significant increase in the accuracy of the forecast, with the mostly comparable results for various advance times, with quantitative estimates of 0.4–0.5 TECU for MAE, 0.6–1.0 TECU for RMSE, 5–7% for MAPE. The same estimates were obtained for three stations along the 30° E meridian.

Keywords: Total Electron Content · Ionosphere · Forecasting · BiGRU · BiLSTM · BiTCN · Temporal Convolution

1 Introduction

The ionosphere is an environment which state is largely determined by space weather, the study of which is devoted to a large number of international projects (e.g., [1, 2]). The authors of the papers [3, 4] note the close relationship between applied geophysics and artificial intelligence technologies. Much attention has traditionally been paid to the use of artificial intelligence methods in the study and forecasting of the main parameter of the ionosphere, the critical frequency, which is associated with the maximum electron density of NmF2 (e.g., [5]).

© The Author(s), under exclusive license to Springer Nature Switzerland AG 2023
B. Shishkov and A. Lazarov (Eds.): ICTRS 2023, CCIS 1990, pp. 33–50, 2023.
https://doi.org/10.1007/978-3-031-49263-1_3

A huge number of applications, such as satellite telecommunications systems and positioning services, actualize the problem of research and forecast of another parameter of ionosphere - total electronic content (e.g., [6]). To solve those problems, a variety of different approaches to forecasting is employed. As is known, there are several types of forecasts: long-term, medium-, short-term (e.g., [7]). This work refers to the use and development of short-term forecast methods. Currently, the most widely used methods are related to machine learning, including neural networks with different architectures [3]. Among the differences between these methods, one of the most important parameters in practice is forecast advance time, and its spread is very large. The most common are periods of forecasting within a day range 1, 2, 6,..., 24 h ahead, and they can be related to the resolution of the available data. This paper uses forecasting periods of 2 and 24 h. The 2 h period is associated with the use of Global Ionospheric Maps IGS [8], which are the most commonly used data source, and are of great importance for areas with the insufficient GPS coverage. In this research, the maps with a resolution of 2 h are used. Among the types of forecast, the daily forecasts are the most common. Therefore, this paper includes a review of methods with 24-h advance times, focusing on the accuracy of the forecasting. In individual articles, it is not often possible to find a comparison of results for different advance periods. In this paper, we intend to compare the results for periods of 2 and 24 h.

Table 1 provides a selection of the statistical results of the previous researches by different authors on the TEC forecast using the most modern methods. At the same time, one should point to the milestone obtained in [9], in which the Standard Persistence Model (SPM) [10] has showed a better result in the 24-h forecast than the widely used and quite effective methods MediMod (a model using a monthly or 27 day median TEC), Fourier series expansion, the Neustrelitz Total Electron Content Model (NTCM-GL) [11]. The forecast was performed for year 2015 and 4 points with latitudes 30°N, 40°N, 50°N, 60°N and longitude 15°E, with the following Root Mean Square Error (RMSE) values respectively: 4.94 TECU, 3.30 TECU, 2.66 TECU, 2.44 TECU. The first column shows the number of the block of results obtained in the papers listed in the last column R, i.e., the first rows represent the results from [12]. The second column contains the names of the architectures. The third column shows the advance time. The fourth and fifth columns contain accuracy evaluation indicators such as Mean Absolute Error (MAE) and RMSE. The sixth column represents the indices used as additional input data. The next column indicates the region. The results are from 13 sources [12–24]. The first 8 groups represent results with advance time of $\tau = 24$ h. Groups 9–10 compare the prediction accuracy for different times τ 24 h and 1 h. Group 11 presents results for $\tau = 2$ h. Group 12 refers to $\tau = 1$ h.

The first two groups have statistical characteristics averaged over many stations of the globe. Groups 3–11 represent results for individual stations. The results of groups 12–13 are derived from IGS map data. Within groups with multiple architectures, it is possible to determine which architectures add an improvement to the prediction. It is also possible to compare global scale results with station-specific data and results of the same architectures for different stations.

Some details are summarized as follows. In the group 1, globally, the bidirectional algorithm did not give an advantage over the unidirectional long term memory LSTM

Table 1. Comparison of accuracy evaluation indicators.

N	Method	τ	MAE	RMS	Index	Region	R
1	LSTM	d	0.8–2.2	–	–	global	12
	Bi-LSTM	d	0.8–2.2	–	–	global	12
	CNN-GRU	d	0.8–1.8	–	–	global	12
	RNN	d	0.9–1.8	–	–	global	12
2	Conv LSTM	d	1.4, 3.27	1.93, 4.66	–	global	13
	PredRNN	d	1.01, 3.14	1.38, 4.35	–	global	13
	ST-LSTM	d	0.88, 2.83	1.2, 3.93	–	global	13
3	LSTM	d	–	3.5	F10.7, ap	Beijing	14
4	Bi-LSTM	d	–	3.35	F10.7, ap	Beijing	15
5	Bi-LSTM	d	–	1–3.5?	F10.7, Kp	India	16
6	LSTM	d	1.53	2.25	Bz, Kp, Dst, F10.7	China	17
	CNN-LSTM	d	1.36	2.07	Bz, Kp, Dst, F10.7	China	17
	CNN-LSTM-Att	d	1.17	1.87	Bz, Kp, Dst, F10.7	China	17
7	BP-NN	d	2.74	3.99	F10.7, SSN	Athens	18
	GA-BP-NN	d	2.11	3.51	F10.7, SSN	Athens	18
	MMAdapGA-BP-NN	d	2.03	2.84	F10.7, SSN	Athens	18
8	LSTM	d	–	2.055	SSN, Kp, F10.7, Dst	Kenya	19
	GRU	d	–	2.004	SSN, Kp, F10.7, Dst	Kenya	19
	MLP	d	–	3.336	SSN, Kp, F10.7, Dst	Kenya	19
9	Random Forest	d	–	1.06,1.86,2.2	–	70–40-10°N	20
	Random Forest	1		0.54, 0.92, 1.2	–	70–40-10°N	20
10	PCA-MRM	d	2.0	2.8	23 indices	Portug	21
	PCA-MRM	1	1.8	4.27	23 indices	Portug	21
11	LSTM	2	1.39	1.85	Dst, IMF, Np, F10.7	Julius	22
	GRU	2	1.5	1.9	Dst, IMF, Np, F10.7	Julius	22
12	Conv LSTM	2	–	1.73	–	IGS	23
	Conv LSTM	1	–	1.43	–	IGS	23
13	LSTM	1	2.721	3.806	R, F10.7, Ap, Dst	IGS	24
	MSAP	1	2.116	3.033	R, F10.7, Ap, Dst	IGS	24

[12]. In the group 2, the first values refer to the minimum of solar activity (2018) and the second to its maximum (2014) [13]. In the groups 3–6, the use of LSTM together with the bidirectional algorithm and CNN resulted in improved prediction [14–17]. In the group 7, a combined intelligent prediction model (MMAdapGA-BP-NN) based on a multi-mutation, multi-cross adaptive genetic algorithm (MMAdapGA) and a back propagation neural network (BP-NN) was proposed and gave the best results compared to BP-NN and GA-BP-NN methods [18]. In the group 8, the Gated Recurrent Unit GRU architecture had a very small advantage over LSTM [19]. In the group 9, the RMSE for 24 h was twice as large as for 1h. For the disturbed period September 7–10, 2017 and 1 h ahead, RMSEs were 0.73 TECU, 1.31 TECU, and 1.29 TECU for points with latitudes 70° N, 40° N, and 10° N, respectively. For 24h ahead, these values were 1.77 TECU, 3.95 TECU, and 3.95 TECU [20]. Group 10 for 24h refers to the prediction of daily mean values. The difference from all the papers is the use of such external indices as the solar UV and XR fluxes, the number of the solar flares of different classes, in addition to parameters of the solar wind and of the interplanetary magnetic field, and geomagnetic indices. In the group 11, the paper [22] is one of two papers in which the MAPE values are given. In particular, they were equal to 14% for LSTM and 17% for GRU. The paper [18] gives MAPE values of 20.14% for BP-NN, 16.75% for GA-BP-NN and 14.53% for MMAdapGA-BP-NN. In the group 12, the accuracy for $\tau = 1$ h is higher than for $\tau = 2$ h. In the group 13 when comparing the results of LSTM and GRU) it was noted that the internal storage structure of the GPU is simpler than that of the LSTM, consequently, the speed of the GRU is much faster than that of the LSTM when the model is trained. Overall, since the structures are the same, the training time of the GRU and the LSTM will be different. Comparing the experimental set up of GRU and LSTM it can be deduced that the GRU model takes far less time than LSTM model when the prediction effect is almost the same as LSTM model [24].

Thus, one can see that bidirectional and CNN algorithms lead to an improvement in the TEC prediction compared to the LSTM method. Most of the methods use the solar activity F10.7 and geomagnetic activity Dst indices as input parameters.

The purpose of this work is to complement the methods of the paper [22] with the prospective bidirectional and CNN algorithms and to compare their effectiveness not only for the advance time $\tau = 2$ h, but also for the most common $\tau = 24$ h. To ensure the continuity of the results in terms of comparison, these methods are considered for the Juliusruh station in 2015 and for those three European stations.

2 Data and Methods

The paper proposes and analyzes 10 new architectures of recurrent and convolutional neural networks that are based on LSTM and GRU architectures and temporal convolution. The results are compared with the literature data, across the presented architectures, and for two considered cases of different forecasting advance time. Four stations from the European Region were selected for the verification of the results.

2.1 Experimental Data

The values of global GIM-TEC maps were calculated from IONEX files with a time step of 2 h (ftp://cddis.gsfc.nasa.gov/pub/gps/products/ionex/) for Juliusruh (54.6° N, 14.6° E), Murmansk (69° N, 33° E), Moscow (55.6° N, 37.2° E), Nicosia (35.1° N, 33.2° E). The Central European station Juliusruh was chosen because it is the benchmark used, for example, for a detailed analysis of ionospheric behavior in a series of 10 papers in the journal Geliogeophysical researches [25] and three papers in the journal Geomagnetism and Aeronomy [26]. The data on the indices of solar and geomagnetic activity Dst, F10.7, IMF, proton density Np and planetary 10Kp index, solar wind speed Vsw was taken from SPDF OMNIWeb Service (http://omniweb.gsfc.nasa.gov/form/dx1.html). All results were obtained using indices 10Kp, Np, F10.7, Dst, Vsw, i.e. the solar wind speed was added, an index, which in additional study showed correlation coefficients $\rho(\delta TEC\text{-}Vsw)$ with relative deviations δTEC from medians close to the correlation coefficients $\rho(\delta TEC\text{-}Dst)$.

The year 2015 was chosen as a reference year for testing of the proposed deep RNN architectures, because it is highly disturbed and most commonly used for testing in publications (e.g., [21, 23, 27]). The behavior of the basic indices influencing the TEC changes is given in Fig. 1

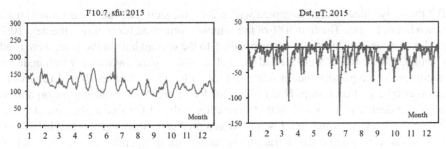

Fig. 1. Average daily values of F10.7 and Dst indices in 2015.

One can see that the solar and geomagnetic activities were higher in the first half of the year. Figure 2 shows the daily mean instantaneous TEC values for Juliusruh, Moscow, Murmansk and Nicosia stations for 2015 to illustrate the response of the ionosphere to geomagnetic disturbances.

The TEC values are numerically close for stations Juliusruh and Moscow. At Murmansk station, the values are slightly lower, and at Nicosia station are higher. One can see that the geomagnetic variations distort a smoother structure provided by solar activity and there is an almost synchronous response of the ionosphere at all stations.

2.2 Data Preparation

The original dataset for 2015 for TEC values and indices included 4380 samples per each variable was split into 3 separate datasets used for training, verification and testing. The time step for TEC values and 10Kp, Np, Dst, Vsw indices was equal to 2 h. For

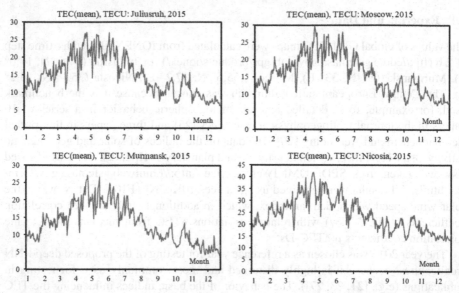

Fig. 2. TEC variations during 2015 for stations Juliusruh, Moscow, Murmansk, Nicosia.

F10.7 the daily values were resampled with a 2-h time step, i.e., the same value is used for each hour of a day. The first 40% of the samples were used for training, the next 10% for validation, and the last 50%, corresponding to the second half of the year, were used for testing. TEC samples were passed through a sliding window with a width equal to 12 samples, forming independent features formed by TEC samples shifted relative to each other by 2 h at each step. Np, 10Kp, Dst, F10.7 and Vsw indices were organized into independent sequences and shifted in relation to the TEC value at the time step t so that the previous index value at $t-1$ was used as a predictor. Since the forecast is built for 2 h ahead and for 24 h ahead, but training is carried out independently, then for each of these cases, the corresponding time delay for the predictors is introduced. For 2-h-ahead forecast the delay was equal to a single time step, and for 24 h ahead forecast the values were delayed by 12 time steps. Data arrays are truncated appropriately to maintain the same array lengths for all features. Thus, the TEC value at the time step t is predicted using 12 delayed previous TEC values and a single previous value of the respective included indices. Error values were replaced with the nearest previous values.

2.3 The Proposed Deep Neural Networks for TEC Forecasting

The proposed architectures can be divided into two main groups: unidirectional and bidirectional. Among these groups, two additional subgroups of architectures can be distinguished, namely, recurrent and convolutional. The same architectures are used to generate forecasts of TEC values for two situations: forecasts for 2 h ahead, and forecasts for 24 h ahead. The notation used is as follows. The postfix "InR" corresponds to the recurrent architecture with the recurrent layer positioned right after the input layer, followed by several fully connected and normalization layers. The postfix "MidR" denotes the recurrent architecture with the recurrent layer placed in the middle of the layer stack. The prefix "Bi" stands for bidirectional architecture, and it can be used with any other designation. If no prefix is used that means the architecture is unidirectional.

Recurrent Neural Networks. Among the variety of architectures of neural networks, recurrent neural networks are most widely used in the tasks of forecasting and modeling time series. However, classical recurrent neural networks are subject to the vanishing gradient problem. For this reason, alternative models have been developed, such as LSTM and GRU, which are used in this paper as building blocks for the deep neural networks development. Long short-term memory networks were introduced in [28]. This architecture consists of an input gate, forget gate, output gate, and it stores the information, learned about the relationships between the timesteps of the input sequence in the internal memory state. The main advantage of LSTM is the ability to handle longer time sequences compared to a conventional recurrent neural network, and its resistance to vanishing gradient problem. An alternative approach to solving a similar problem is based on the use of the Gated Recurrent Unit [29], a simplified modification of the LSTM, lacking cell state and having less gates, which are replaced with a set of control vectors. The elements of the internal structure of these cells and connections are illustrated in Fig. 3.

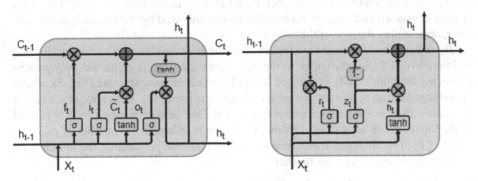

Fig. 3. Structural diagrams of LSTM (left) and GRU (right) cells.

One of the common modifications of recurrent neural networks, such as GRU and LSTM, is based on a principle model called the bidirectional recurrent neural network. This model is formed by two layers of recurrent neural networks that process data in forward and reverse directions, and whose outputs are concatenated or added afterwards (Fig. 4). Architectures of this type are most widely used in natural language processing, but have also been successfully applied to time series forecasting problems, especially in the case of complex nonlinear dependencies, or series or sequential events, which is true for the relationship between TEC values and the solar and geomagnetic indices.

The layer diagrams for the proposed recurrent architectures are given in the Fig. 5. The recurrent layer used (LSTM, GRU, BiLSTM, BiGRU) determines the specific architecture among the corresponding architecture lines. The "InR" line of architectures includes a single recurrent layer, placed after the input layer, and followed by a batch normalization layer, then one fully connected layer, another batch normalization

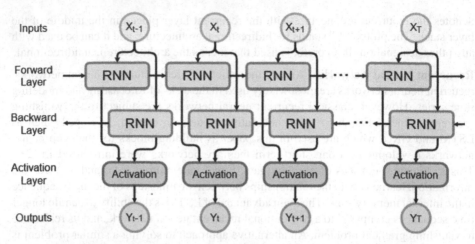

Fig. 4. Schematic representation of a bidirectional neural network.

layer, then two fully connected layer, last of which determines the size of the output. The "MidR" line of architectures includes a fully connected layer, placed after the input layer, and followed by a recurrent layer, then by a batch normalization layer, and two pairs of fully connected and batch normalization layers, followed by the last fully connected layer, determining the size of the output.

By default, the input and recurrent weights are initialized using the Xavier Glorot's initialization [30]. Same applies to the fully connected layers, with the only exception being the middle fully connected layer of the InR architecture line (Fig. 5), where the orthogonal matrix decomposition initialization is used [31]. The sigmoid activation function is used as the gate activation function and the tanh activation function is used as the internal state activation function. The value N indicates the number of processing cells used in the layer. Batch normalization layers are performing the per-channel normalization across the mini-batches.

Convolutional Neural Networks. Convolutional neural networks are an actively developing and widespread type of neural networks used in areas such as image and voice recognition and generation, sound and language processing. Depending on the dimensionality of the problem, convolutional neural networks are divided into 1-dimensional, 2-dimensional, etc. For time series forecasting problems, an effective solution is a modification of one-dimensional convolutional neural networks, called a temporal convolutional neural network, a distinctive feature of which is the inherent deep learning capability, due to the use of a series of filters with different time shifts, called the dilation factors, combined with the causal padding [32]. For a sample s the convolution F with the dilation factor d and the kernel size k is defined as:

$$F(s) = (x *_d f)(s) = \sum_{i=0}^{k-1} f(i) \cdot x_{s-d \cdot i}. \tag{1}$$

The proposed unidirectional and bidirectional temporal convolutional networks consisted of a series of single-dimension convolution layers with causal padding applied,

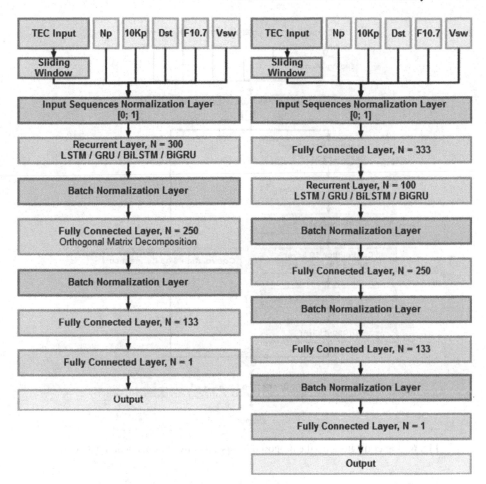

Fig. 5. Layer diagrams for the proposed InR (left) and MidR (right) deep neural network architectures. The selected recurrent layer is defined at the level of a specific architecture of a given family of architectures.

stacked in their respective branches. The temporal convolution is implemented using the dilation factor equal to 1 in the first convolution 1D layer, and the dilation factor equal to 12 in the following convolution 1D layer. The number of filters was equal to 256 with a filter kernel size equal to 6. The weights in the convolution 1D layers are initialized using Glorot's initialization. Two batch normalization layers were included after each convolution 1D layers, followed by dropout layers with a dropout factor of 0.005, forming the forward processing branch. Additionally, the convolution skip connection was included for stabilization and learning time improvement, as the information from the original input is passed through the network. The outputs for each branch were connected using addition connection. The layer diagram for the proposed unidirectional TCN is given in Fig. 6.

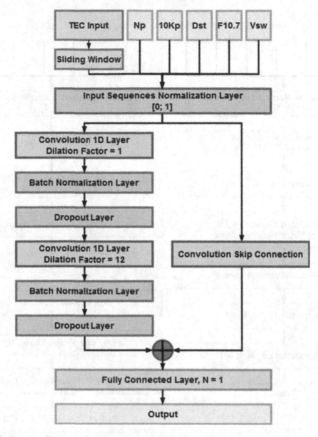

Fig. 6. Layer diagram for the proposed temporal convolutional neural network.

The bidirectional temporal convolutional neural network (BiTCN) is created using the same approach as for the bidirectional recurrent neural networks, however, the recurrent layers are replaced by the entire forward processing branch, supplemented by two flip layers at the beginning and end of the branch, inverting the order of inputs and outputs. Convolution skip connection was also included in parallel. The layer diagram of the proposed bidirectional temporal convolutional network is presented in Fig. 7.

2.4   Training Parameters

The input data for every considered architecture was normalized using per-channel rescaling in the range from 0 to 1, i.e., the minimum value for each individual feature was zero, and the maximum value was equal to one.

Mean Squared Error was used as the loss function during the training:

$$loss = \frac{1}{n} \sum_{i=1}^{n} \left(\widehat{TEC}_{pre,i} - TEC_{obs,i} \right)^2, \tag{2}$$

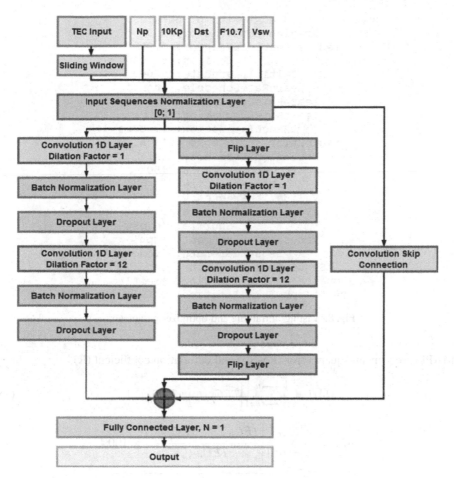

Fig. 7. Layer diagram for the proposed bidirectional temporal convolutional neural network.

where *n* is the number of samples.

The training was performed using MATLAB environment and Deep Learning and Parallel Computing Toolboxes. For each considered architecture, the same set of training and optimized parameters is used. Initial learning rate was equal to 0.003. The networks are trained for 150 epochs. The stochastic gradient descent method that is based on adaptive estimation of first-order and second-order moments (ADAM) was used as an optimizer. A detailed list of parameters is given in Fig. 8.

2.5 Forecasting Accuracy Metrics

The comparison of the forecasting accuracy for different architectures is performed using a set of metrics, including Mean Absolute Error (MAE), Mean Absolute Percentage Error

```
TrainingOptionsADAM with properties:
          GradientDecayFactor: 0.9000
   SquaredGradientDecayFactor: 0.9990
                      Epsilon: 1.0000e-08
              InitialLearnRate: 0.0030
            LearnRateSchedule: 'none'
          LearnRateDropFactor: 0.1000
          LearnRateDropPeriod: 10
              L2Regularization: 1.0000e-04
        GradientThresholdMethod: 'l2norm'
            GradientThreshold: Inf
                    MaxEpochs: 150
                MiniBatchSize: 1
          ValidationFrequency: 20
            ValidationPatience: Inf
                      Shuffle: 'every-epoch'
          ExecutionEnvironment: 'gpu'
              SequenceLength: 'longest'
          SequencePaddingValue: 0
      SequencePaddingDirection: 'left'
        ResetInputNormalization: 0
```

Fig. 8. Listing of training and optimizer parameters.

(MAPE), root-mean-square error (RMSE) and correlation coefficient (R):

$$MAE = \frac{1}{n} \sum_{i=1}^{n} \left| \widehat{TEC}_{pre,i} - TEC_{obs,i} \right|, \tag{3}$$

$$MAPE = \frac{1}{n} \sum_{i=1}^{n} \left| \frac{\widehat{TEC}_{pre,i} - TEC_{obs,i}}{TEC_{obs,i}} \right| \times 100\%, \tag{4}$$

$$RMSE = \sqrt{\sum_{i=1}^{n} \frac{\left(\widehat{TEC}_{pre,i} - TEC_{obs,i} \right)^2}{n}}, \tag{5}$$

$$R = \frac{cov\left(TEC_{obs}, \widehat{TEC}_{pre} \right)}{\sigma_{TEC_{obs}} \cdot \sigma_{\widehat{TEC}_{pre}}}. \tag{6}$$

3   Results and Discussion

The statistical results on accuracy of TEC forecasting for a set of 10 considered architectures are presented in Table 2. The metrics considered were MAE, MAPE, RMSE, R, averaged over half a year during a single step forecasting.

To enhance clarity and facilitate analysis, the results of the table are shown in Fig. 9 in the form of diagrams for each statistical indicator (3 graphs) and a graph of indicator ratios for periods 2 h and 24 h: Ratio = Ind(2 h)/Ind(24 h). This ratio shows how many

Table 2. Forecasting results for Juliusruh station in 2015.

	Juliusruh	MAE, TECU		MAPE, %		RMSE, TECU		ρ	
	2015	2 h	24 h	2 h	24 h	2 h	24 h	2 h	24 h
1	LSTM-MidR	1.443	4.792	15.091	50.450	1.942	6.278	0.96	0.84
2	LSTM-InR	1.274	2.361	13.521	26.366	1.819	3.178	0.96	0.92
3	GRU-MidR	1.364	4.992	13.227	49.743	1.896	6.364	0.97	0.83
4	GRU-InR	1.161	3.625	11.722	36.594	1.601	4.638	0.97	0.89
5	TCN	1.173	2.277	12.807	25.746	1.616	3.006	0.97	0.88
6	BiLSTM-MidR	0.228	1.376	3.640	16.185	0.345	1.840	1.00	0.96
7	BiLSTM-InR	0.475	1.006	5.522	12.008	0.806	1.562	0.99	0.97
8	BiGRU-MidR	0.236	1.109	4.019	13.183	0.446	1.521	1.00	0.97
9	BiGRU-InR	0.389	0.997	4.734	10.963	0.631	1.358	0.99	0.98
10	BiTCN	0.433	0.507	5.195	6.887	0.625	1.083	0.99	0.98

times the efficiency of this architecture for a 24 h forecast is worse than the efficiency for a 2 h forecast.

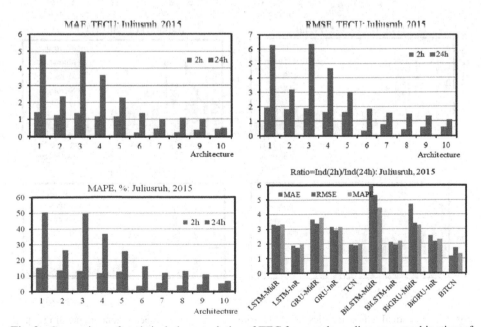

Fig. 9. Comparison of statistical characteristics of TEC forecast depending on a combination of architecture and the advance time.

If to consider separately the results for 2 h advance time, it can be seen that the first five architectures provide approximately the same level of MAE accuracy (with a minor improvement with increasing architecture number in accordance with RMSE). The implementation of the bidirectional model significantly improves the accuracy for architectures 6–10 with the best result achieved by the architecture 6 (BiLSTM-MidR). For 24 h advance time, the significant differences for LSTM with MidR and InR modifications (architectures 1–2) are observed, as well as for GRU (architectures 3–4). The bidirectional processing algorithm leads to the major improvement in the accuracy. For architecture 10 (BiTCN) the accuracy for 2 h and 24 h advance times is comparable for MAE and MAPE, but is 2 times lower for 24 h in terms of RMSE. Overall, the best result for both considered advance times was obtained for the BiTCN architecture. The Ratio graph shows how many times the efficiency of a particular architecture for a 24 h forecast is worse than for a 2 h forecast.

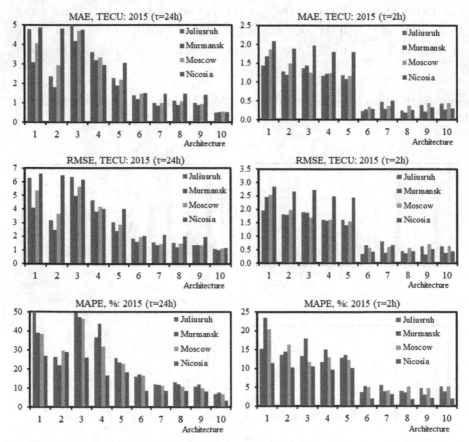

Fig. 10. Statistical characteristics of TEC forecast in the European zone depending on a combination of architecture and the advance time.

The results for every station considered are shown in Fig. 10 as a dependence of MAE, MAPE and RMSE on the architecture's variant number. Thus, the results are presented for the following architectures, indicated by numbers: (1) LSTM-MidR, (2) LSTM-InR, (3) GRU-MidR, (4) GRU-InR, (5) TCN, (6) BiLSTM-MidR, (7) BiLSTM-InR, (8) BiGRU-MidR, (9) BiGRU-InR, (10) BiTCN.

The results for the Juliusruh station make it possible to analyze the situation for the remaining stations by a simple comparison. Thus, it can be seen that the results for Moscow station are closest to the results for Juliusruh station, while for Murmansk and Nicosia stations they can be either better or worse than for Juliusruh, but with almost the same ratios between architecture efficiency and accuracies for 2 h and 24 h, however, one can also see certain latitudinal differences within one particular architecture.

The forecast errors during the second half of each year for the Moscow station are shown in Fig. 11. The left panel shows the variations of TEC between DoY 185 and 365 along with the Dst index, the middle panel shows the errors for BiLSTM-MidR during the 2 h advance time forecast, and the right panel shows the errors for BiTCN for 24 h advance time forecast.

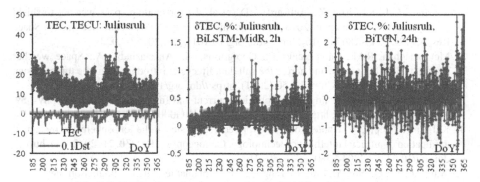

Fig. 11. TEC values for the second half of 2015 and forecast errors.

4 Conclusion

In this paper, the effectiveness of recurrent and convolutional models was studied for 10 different presented architectures: (1) (1) LSTM-MidR, (2) LSTM-InR, (3) GRU-MidR, (4) GRU-InR, (5) TCN, (6) BiLSTM-MidR, (7) BiLSTM-InR, (8) BiGRU-MidR, (9) BiGRU-InR, (10) BiTCN. We used TEC data from four European stations (Juliusruh, Murmansk, Moscow, Nicosia) for year 2015. The main attention is paid to comparing the forecast accuracy for advance times of 2 h and 24 h. Table 1, which presents the literature data, shows that most of the results are comparable to the estimates of Methods 1–5. Methods 6–10 associated with the implementation of bidirectional model provide a significant improvement in forecasting accuracy. This can be seen, in particular, when compared with the results of [22], which are the starting points for this work. Even the Random Forest method [20], which doubles the forecast efficiency when moving from

24 h to 1 h, does not reach the level of using bidirectional algorithms in combination with LSTM, GRU, and TCN. On average, quantitative estimates for all stations during 24 h advance time are reduced to 0.4–0.5 TECU for MAE, 0.6–1.0 TECU for RMSE, 5–7% for MAPE for the presented bidirectional architectures. In conclusion, it should be noted that the calculations were performed using a computer having the following characteristics: GPU: NVIDIA *GeForce RTX 4080*; CPU: AMD Ryzen 9 7900X; 32 GB RAM. To train network at one station for 150 epochs the required time is: for BiGRU/BiLSTM-MidR—~20 s, for BiGRU/BiLSTM-InR—~25 s, for BiTCN—~5 s.

Acknowledgments. The authors are grateful to the developers of websites: http://omniweb.gsfc.nasa.gov/form/dx1.html, ftp://cddis.gsfc.nasa.gov/pub/gps/products/ionex/. The research was financially supported by Ministry of Science and Higher Education of the Russian Federation (State task in the field of scientific activity 2023).

References

1. Schrijver, C.J., Kauristie, K., Aylward, A.D., et al.: Understanding space weather to shield society: a global road map for 2015–2025 commissioned by COSPAR and ILWS. Adv. Space Res. **55**(12), 2745–2807 (2015). https://doi.org/10.1016/j.asr.2015.03.023
2. McGranaghan, R.M., Camporeale, E., Georgoulis, M., Anastasiadis, A.: Space weather research in the digital age and across the full data lifecycle: introduction to the topical issue. J. Space Weather Space Clim. **11**, 50 (2021). https://doi.org/10.1051/swsc/2021037
3. Yu, S., Ma, J.: Deep learning for geophysics: current and future trends. Rev. Geophys. **59**, e2021RG000742 (2021). https://doi.org/10.1029/2021RG000742
4. Kalinin, Y., Repin, A., Khotenko, E.N.: Applied geophysics of the ionosphere and the actual application of artificial intelligence technology. Geliogeophys. Res. **30**, 21–29 (2021). https://doi.org/10.54252/2304-7380_2021_30_21
5. Wang, J., Yu, Q., Shi, Y., Liu, Y., Yang, C.: An explainable dynamic prediction method for ionospheric foF2 based on machine learning. Remote Sens. **15**, 1256 (2023). https://doi.org/10.3390/rs15051256
6. Xie, T., Dai, Z., Zhu, X., Chen, B., Ran, C.: LSTM-based short-term ionospheric TEC forecast model and positioning accuracy analysis. GPS Solutions **27**, 66 (2023). https://doi.org/10.1007/s10291-023-01406-8
7. Nishioka, M., Saito, S., Tao, C., Shiota, D., Tsugawa, T., Ishii, M.: Statistical analysis of ionospheric total electron content (TEC): long-term estimation of extreme TEC in Japan Earth. Planets Space **73**(52), 1–12 (2021). https://doi.org/10.1186/s40623-021-01374-8
8. Hernández-Pajares, M., et al.: The IGS VTEC maps: a reliable source of ionospheric information since 1998. J. Geod. **83**, 263–275 (2009)
9. Badeke, R., Borries, C., Hoque, M.M., Minkwitz, D.: Empirical forecast of quiet time ionospheric total electron content maps over Europe. Adv. Space Res. **61**, 2881–2890 (2018). https://doi.org/10.1016/j.asr.2018.04.010
10. Garcia-Rigo, A., et al.: Global prediction of the vertical total electron content of the ionosphere based on GPS data. Radio Sci. **46**, RS0D25 (2011). https://doi.org/10.1029/2010RS004643
11. Jakowski, N., Hoque, M.M., Mayer, C.: A new global TEC model for estimating transionospheric radio wave propagation errors. J. Geod. **85**, 965–974 (2011). https://doi.org/10.1007/s00190-011-0455-1

12. Kaselimi, M., Voulodimos, A., Doulamis, N., Doulamis, A., Delikaraoglou, D.: Deep recurrent neural networks for ionospheric variations estimation using GNSS measurements. IEEE Trans. Geosci. Remote Sens. **60**, 1–15 (2022). https://doi.org/10.1109/TGRS.2021.3090856
13. Lin, X., et al.: A spatiotemporal network model for global ionospheric TEC forecasting. Remote Sens. **14**, 1717 (2022). https://doi.org/10.3390/rs14071717
14. Sun, W., et al.: Forecasting of ionospheric vertical total electron content (TEC) using LSTM networks. In: Proceedings of the 2017 International Conference on Machine Learning and Cybernetics, Ningbo, China, 9–12 July 2017
15. Sun, W., Xu, L., Huang, X., Zhang, W., Yuan, T., Yan, Y.: Bidirectional LSTM for ionospheric vertical total electron content (TEC) forecasting. In: Proceedings of IEEE Vision and Communication Image Processing (VCIP), December 2017, pp. 1–4 (2017). https://doi.org/10.1109/VCIP.2017.8305097
16. Sivakrishna, K., Ratnam, D.V., Sivavaraprasad, G.: A bidirectional deep-learning algorithm to forecast regional ionospheric TEC maps. IEEE J. Sel. Top. Appl. Earth Observ. Remote Sens. **15**, 4531–4543 (2022). https://doi.org/10.1109/JSTARS.2022.3180940
17. Tang, J., Li, Y., Ding, M., Liu, H., Yang, D., Wu, X.: An ionospheric TEC forecasting model based on a CNN-LSTM-attention mechanism neural network. Remote Sens. **14**, 2433 (2022). https://doi.org/10.3390/rs14102433
18. Weng, J., Liu, Y., Wang, J.: A model-assisted combined machine learning method for ionospheric TEC prediction. Remote Sens. **15**, 2953 (2023). https://doi.org/10.3390/rs15122953
19. Iluore, K., Lu, J.: Long short-term memory and gated recurrent neural networks to predict the ionospheric vertical total electron content. Adv. Space Res. **70**, 652–665 (2022). https://doi.org/10.1016/j.asr.2022.04.066
20. Natras, R., Soja, B., Schmidt, M.: Ensemble machine learning of random forest, AdaBoost and XGBoost for vertical total electron content forecasting. Remote Sens. **14**(3547), 1–34 (2022). https://doi.org/10.3390/rs14153547
21. Morozova, A.L., Barata, T., Barlyaeva, T.: PCA-MRM model to forecast TEC at middle latitudes. Atmosphere **13**, 323 (2022). https://doi.org/10.3390/atmos13020323
22. Kharakhashyan, A., Maltseva, O., Glebova, G.: Forecasting the total electron content TEC of the ionosphere using space weather parameters. In: Proceedings of the 2021 IEEE International Conference on Wireless for Space and Extreme Environments (WiSEE), Cleveland, OH, USA, 12–14 October 2021, pp. 31–36 (2021). https://doi.org/10.1109/WiSEE50203.2021.9613829
23. Chen, J., Zhi, N., Liao, H., Lu, M., Feng, S.: Global forecasting of ionospheric vertical total electron contents via ConvLSTM with spectrum analysis. GPS Solutions **26**, 69 (2022). https://doi.org/10.1007/s10291-022-01253-z
24. Chen, Z., Liao, W., Li, H., Wang, J., Deng, X., Hong, S.: Prediction of global ionospheric TEC based on deep learning. Space Weather **20**, e2021SW002854 (2022). https://doi.org/10.1029/2021SW002854
25. Danilov, A.D., Konstantinova, A.V.: Detailed analysis of the behavior of the F2-layer critical frequency prior to magnetic storms. 10. Proportion between negative and positive events. Geliogeophys. Res. **35**, 3–11 (2022). https://doi.org/10.5425/2304-7380_2022_35_3
26. Danilov, A.D., Konstantinova, A.V.: Ionospheric precursors of magnetic storms. 3. Analysis of juliusruh station data. Geomagn. Aeron. (Engl. Transl.) **61**(3), 341–348 (2021). https://doi.org/10.1134/S0016793221030087
27. Ren, X., Yang, P., Liu, H., Chen, J., Liu, W.: Deep learning for global ionospheric TEC forecasting: different approaches and validation. Space Weather **20**, e2021SW003011 (2022). https://doi.org/10.1029/2021SW003011
28. Hochreiter, S., Schmidhuber, J.: Long short-term memory neural computation. Neural Comput. **9**(8), 1735–1780 (1997). https://doi.org/10.1162/neco.1997.9.8.1735

29. Cho, K., et al.: Learning phrase representations using RNN encoder-decoder for statistical machine translation. arXiv:1406.1078v3 [cs.CL] 3, (2014). https://arxiv.org/pdf/1406.1078.pdf
30. Glorot, X., Bengio, Y.: Understanding the difficulty of training deep feedforward neural networks. In: Proceedings of the Thirteenth International Conference on Artificial Intelligence and Statistics, Sardinia, Italy: AISTATS, pp. 249–356 (2010)
31. Saxe, A.M., McClelland, J.L., Ganguli, S.: Exact solutions to the nonlinear dynamics of learning in deep linear neural networks. arXiv preprint arXiv:1312.6120 (2013)
32. Bai, S., Kolter, J.Z., Koltun, J.V.: An empirical evaluation of generic convolutional and recurrent networks for sequence modelling, 19 April, pp. 1–14 (2018, preprint, submitted). https://arxiv.org/abs/1803.01271

A Public-Key System Based on Primes and Addition

Rodney H. Cooper[1]([✉]) [iD], Jeff Retallick[2] [iD], and Brent R. Petersen[1] [iD]

[1] University of New Brunswick, Fredericton, NB, Canada
morbius@unb.ca
[2] Employed in the private sector, Calgary, AB, Canada

Abstract. In this paper, we describe a public-key algorithm that uses random primes to construct a matrix that is made public. To encrypt an integer, say P, representing a given plaintext message, the integer P is used to select a unique set of integers S from this constructed matrix. To encrypt the message, the integers in the set S are added, and the resulting sum represents the encrypted message. To decrypt the message, three secret keys are used in a mathematical algorithm to determine the original message P from the sum.

Keywords: public-key cryptography · Pascal triangle · prime numbers · addition

1 Preliminary Steps

In this algorithm, a mapping is constructed to convert a plaintext message P to a ciphertext message C [1]. This mapping can be represented as $E : P \to C$ where E is the *encryption* mapping. In this paper, we shall assume that both the domain and the codomain of the mapping E is the set of non-negative integers $\mathbb{Z}^{0+}$. How a plaintext message will be converted to an integer is left to the user's discretion. In the nineteenth century, when much business was conducted by the sending and receiving of telegrams, codebooks of integers were often used to replace combinations of words. One such codebook, for example, used 150 to replace the phrase *Will abide by*. From this point forward, we will assume that the plaintext message P is simply an integer.

The algorithm described in this paper uses the message P to determine a set of integers stored as elements of a publicly available matrix designated as PK. The letters P and K stand for *Public Key*, and this matrix PK is the public key of this algorithm. How this matrix PK is constructed will be discussed later in Sect. 2.2. Assuming that we have already constructed this matrix of integers PK and the integer message P, we first describe how P is used to choose elements from the matrix PK.

Since this algorithm has several steps, the algorithm will first be explained using a small toy example, and the numbers will be kept small. Later in the paper, we will discuss practical issues, and much larger numbers will be involved.

© The Author(s), under exclusive license to Springer Nature Switzerland AG 2023
B. Shishkov and A. Lazarov (Eds.): ICTRS 2023, CCIS 1990, pp. 51–64, 2023.
https://doi.org/10.1007/978-3-031-49263-1_4

Given a plaintext integer P, the encryption process will begin by converting P into a set S of integers whose sum must add up to P. Of course, there are many ways of doing this. For example, the integer 150 could be first translated into binary as 1001 0110. Writing this as powers of 2 yields $2^7 + 2^4 + 2^2 + 2 = 128 + 16 + 4 + 2$ which adds up to 150, giving the set $S = \{128, 16, 4, 2\}$. One convenient result of using the powers of 2 is that any person who knows the algorithm for converting from decimal integers to binary can find the same integers. The details are shown in Algorithm 1.

Algorithm 1: Converting to binary

Data: a non-negative integer n in base 10
Result: a set of numbers which add to n

1 if $n = 0$ then
2 | return 0
3 | exit the algorithm
4 end
5 repeat
6 | Calculate the largest value of j such that $2^j \leq n$
7 | Output 2^j
8 | Calculate $n = n - 2^j$
9 until $n = 0$
10 exit the algorithm

Since the numbers chosen in this article are stored in the public matrix PK and must be chosen based on the plaintext integer P, we need an algorithm for choosing which integers to select from the matrix PK. This is a two-step process. In the first step, it is necessary to construct an $m \times m$ *preliminary* matrix we shall call PM. This matrix PM must have the same dimensions as the matrix PK. There is a unique matrix PM for every size depending on the value of m. For illustration purposes, suppose that PK is a 6×6 matrix. In this case, the matrix PM is

$$PM = \begin{bmatrix} 1 & 1 & 1 & 1 & 1 & 1 \\ 6 & 5 & 4 & 3 & 2 & 1 \\ \mathbf{21} & 15 & 10 & 6 & 3 & 1 \\ \mathbf{56} & \mathbf{35} & 20 & 10 & 4 & 1 \\ 126 & 70 & 35 & 15 & 5 & 1 \\ 252 & 126 & 56 & 21 & 6 & 1 \end{bmatrix}. \tag{1}$$

A matrix of any size can be made in exactly the same manner as this one. The first row and last column consist only of 1 s. Every other cell in the matrix consists of the sum of the integer in the cell directly above it and the entry in the cell directly on its right. For example, $PM[4, 1] = 56$ is the sum of the two integers $PM[3, 1] = 21$ in the row directly above and $PM[4, 2] = 35$ in the same row to its right; see the integers boldfaced in equation (1). In general, for any $m \times m$ matrix PM, the entry $PM[r, c]$ for any row, r, $r > 1$ and any column, c, $c < m$, is given by

$$PM[r, c] = PM[r - 1, c] + PM[r, c + 1]. \tag{2}$$

Using this preliminary matrix PM, we can find yet another set S of integers that sum to 150. The integers in the set S that sum to an integer n are known as the *addends* of n. The method is somewhat similar to the method used for converting a decimal integer to a binary integer, as shown above. First, examine the entry in the matrix in the bottom left corner. In the example 6×6 case, $PM[6, 1] = 252$. Since this integer is greater than 150, it is ignored. To ignore an integer, move to the integer in the row directly above. In this case, that integer is $PM[5, 1] = 126$. Since this is less than 150, it is chosen and can be placed in the set S, giving $S = \{126\}$. This leaves $150 - 126 = 24$. Whenever an integer is chosen for inclusion in S, move to the right by one column in the same row of the matrix; in this case, that is $PM[5, 2]$. $PM[5, 2] = 70$ which is clearly too big. Ignore it and move to the row directly above in row 4. Unfortunately, $PM[4, 2] = 35$, which is still too big. Once again, ignore it and move to the row directly above, $PM[3, 2] = 15$. Since 15 is less than 24, it is chosen for S, $S = \{126, 15\}$. This leaves $24 - 15 = 9$. Since an integer was chosen for S, move to the right in the matrix at $PM[3, 3]$. It is ignored since $PM[3, 3] = 10$, which is too large. Move directly to the row above, $PM[2, 3] = 4$. This can be chosen and placed in S, $S = \{126, 15, 4\}$. This leaves $9 - 4 = 5$. Moving to the right again, $PM[2, 4] = 3$. This is chosen, $S = \{126, 15, 4, 3\}$ leaving $5 - 3 = 2$. Finally, moving to the right, we find $PM[2, 5] = 2$ and this is added to $S = \{126, 15, 4, 3, 2\}$ leaving zero. At this point, the addends of 150 are the elements of the set S and indeed $126 + 15 + 4 + 3 + 2 = 150$, and the process is complete. The algorithm for finding the integers in S selected from PM is shown in Fig. 1 and Algorithm 2. Finding the addends of the integer 150 has taken a route through the matrix PM beginning at row 6 and column 1 at the bottom left of the matrix and then moving either up a row or across a column in a series of steps until the last addend is found at row 2 and column 1. At each stage, moving is always either to the column on the right of an integer selected for inclusion in S or to the row directly above an integer not selected for inclusion in S.

The amazing thing about this matrix PM is that it has a set of integers that adds up to 150. Surprisingly, 150 is not unique in this respect. The *addends*, those integers whose sum adds up to a given integer, can be found not only for 150 but for all the integers from 0 to 461 using precisely the same algorithm. 461 is one less than the sum of the integers in the last row of PM. This is a mathematical property of the matrix PM because the matrix PM has its elements taken from a subset of the famous Pascal triangle, as seen in Fig. 2. The PM matrix is simply a counterclockwise rotation by $45°$ of the Pascal Triangle.

$$
PM = \begin{bmatrix}
1 & 1 & 1 & 1 & 1 & 1 \\
6 & 5 & 4 \rightarrow & 3 \rightarrow 2 & & 1 \\
21 & 15 \rightarrow & \uparrow & 6 & 3 & 1 \\
56 & \uparrow & 20 & 10 & 4 & 1 \\
126 \rightarrow & \uparrow & 35 & 15 & 5 & 1 \\
\uparrow & 126 & 56 & 21 & 6 & 1
\end{bmatrix}
$$

Fig. 1. The route taken to find the addends of 150 in the matrix PM

Algorithm 2: Converting an integer n to a set of integers in the matrix PM whose sum is n

Data: an integer n in base 10
Result: a set of numbers S taken from the preliminary matrix PM whose sum
is n

1 Given n and $S = \{\}$
2 **if** $n = 0$ **then**
3   Set $S = S \cup \{0\}$
4   **exit the algorithm**
5 **end**
6 *Let e be the next possible entry in PM that can be considered for membership in S*
7 Set $e = PM[m, 1]$ where m is size of the $m \times m$ matrix PM
8 Set $r = m$
9 Set $c = 1$
10 **repeat**
11   **if** $e \leq n$ **then**
12      $S = S \cup \{e\}$
13   Calculate $n = n - e$
14   **if** $n \neq 0$ **then**
15   Set $c = c + 1$
16   Set $e = PM[r, c]$
17   **end**
18   **end**
19   **else**
20   Set $r = r - 1$
21   Set $e = PM[r, c]$
22   **end**
23 **until** $n = 0$
24 **exit the algorithm**

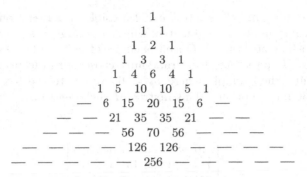

Fig. 2. Pascal's triangle

The Pascal triangle, as is well known, has a myriad of interesting properties. One such property is that the addends of any integer x, $0 \leq x < n$ where n is equal to the sum of the elements in the bottom row of a matrix PM formed by rotating a Pascal Triangle 45° counterclockwise, can be found using Algorithm 2 as described above. Since all the elements of a Pascal triangle of any size are binomial coefficients, a formula for calculating the value of n exists.[1] In an $m \times m$ preliminary matrix PM, the addends of any integer x, $0 < x < n$, satisfies

$$0 \leq x \leq \binom{2m-1}{m-1} - 1. \tag{3}$$

Using the 6×6 matrix PM in the Eq. (1), this property says that the addends for all integers n with $m = 6$ is

$$\binom{2m-1}{m-1} = \binom{2 \times 6 - 1}{6 - 1} = \binom{11}{5} = 462 \tag{4}$$

and hence

$$\&0 \leq n \leq 462 - 1 = 461, \tag{5}$$

as stated previously.

2 Encryption

2.1 Creating the Secret and Public Keys

The first stage in creating the secret and public keys, described in detail in Algorithm 3, is to decide the choice for m in order that all plaintext messages can be included and build the appropriate preliminary $m \times m$ matrix PM. In

---

[1] The sum of the elements in any row m of the rotated Pascal Triangle is the value of the element at position $[m + 1, 1]$ which is $\binom{2m-1}{m-1}$, easily deduced by considering the entries in a Pascal Triangle.

the running example, $m = 6$. There are 462 possible messages, from 0 to 461. In a more practical example, a 6×6 matrix will not be large or secure enough, and m must be much greater than 6. Once the choice of m is made, creating another $m \times m$ matrix M consisting of m^2 randomly chosen **unique** prime integers is next. Continuing the example where $m = 6$, we create the 6×6 matrix M consisting of 36 unique primes. This matrix M is chosen to be

$$
M = \begin{bmatrix}
797 & 887 & 683 & 307 & 541 & 353 \\
761 & 379 & 263 & 431 & 521 & 211 \\
739 & 239 & 811 & 367 & 907 & 167 \\
719 & 743 & 419 & 557 & 503 & 701 \\
857 & 131 & 839 & 293 & 227 & 251 \\
223 & 199 & 631 & 359 & 571 & 103
\end{bmatrix}. \tag{6}
$$

This matrix M should never be revealed and is the first *secret key*.

The second secret key is a prime integer; call it p. This prime p must have more digits than $m - 1$ times the number of digits in the largest prime found in M. In this case, the largest prime, 907, has three digits; thus, the prime must have greater than $(6 - 1) \times 3 = 15$ digits, but it could have, if you so choose, even more than 16 digits. In this case, we choose

$$
p = 26\,539\,967\,940\,317\,371 \tag{7}
$$

which is a 17-digit prime. The third and final secret key is a primitive root of p, which we can designate as g. In this example, we set

$$
g = 4\,382\,133\,298\,784\,737. \tag{8}
$$

The final construction before we can begin the process of encryption is to create another matrix, call it PK of the same size as M, but which contains all the discrete logarithms of the entries found in M using the primitive root g and the prime p. This new matrix PK is made public. Recall that PK stands for public key.

Because the entries are large, the actual matrix cannot be shown. Some elements of the 6×6 PK matrix are illustrated in Eqs. (9) to (13).

2.2   Encrypting

To send a *plaintext* message, the process is undemanding. First, the addends of the message are found from the matrix PM; but this time, we do not need the addends themselves, but rather the addresses of the locations where the addends are found in the matrix PM. Next, the entries at these very same locations are located in the matrix PK. These entries are summed, and the resulting total represents the *ciphertext* message C.

Algorithm 3: Creating the secret and private keys, and the process of encrypting

---

Data: The dimensions of the matrices chosen for this algorithm will, in turn, determine the maximum size of plaintext messages.

Result: The three secret keys, the public key, and the method of encrypting

Build the preliminary matrix PM

1 First, determine a maximum upper bound for the number of integers this algorithm can encrypt and decrypt given the dimensions $m \times m$ of the matrices to be used.

2 Create the preliminary matrix PM from the Pascal triangle of size $m \times m$ where $\binom{2m-1}{m-1} = n - 1$. A preliminary matrix of this size will enable the addends of all n integers x to be found where $0 \le x \le n - 1$.

Build the secret matrix M

3 Build an $m \times m$ matrix M consisting of m^2 **unique** primes chosen randomly.

Determine the secret prime p *and a primitive root* g *of* p

4 Determine the largest prime in the matrix M and determine the number of digits it contains. Call this d.

5 Choose a prime p whose number of digits is d_{prime} such that $d_{prime} > (m - 1) \times d$.

6 Find a random primitive root g of the prime p.

Build the $m \times m$ *public-key matrix* PK

7 Build an $m \times m$ matrix PK consisting of the discrete $\log_g(M[i,j]) \mod p$ of each entry in the matrix M such that $PK[i,j] = \log_g(M[i,j]) \mod p$, where i and j are the indices of both PK and M.

The method of encryption

8 Find the locations of the addends in the integer P representing the plaintext from the preliminary matrix PM. Sum the entries in the public matrix PK at the very same locations where the addends of the plaintext were found in PM and store this sum in the variable C. The integer C is the encryption representing the ciphertext.

Let us continue with the example. Assume the plaintext message is 150. The addends of 150 are $\{126, 15, 4, 3, 2\}$, as discovered in Sect. 1. We are not interested in the addends themselves. Only knowing where they are found in the matrix PM is essential. As stated in Sect. 1, the locations are $PM[5,1]$ for addend 126, $PM[3,2]$ for addend 15, $PM[2,3]$ for addend 4, $PM[2,4]$ for addend 3, and finally $PM[2,5]$ for addend 2. To encrypt 150, we select the entries at the very same positions, namely at locations [5,1], [3,2], [2,3], [2,4], and [2,5], but this time in the public matrix PK. Although the matrix in the running example itself is too large to display, these particular entries and their sum are as follows:

$$PK[5,1] = 8\,912\,850\,277\,394\,241 \tag{9}$$

$$PK[3,2] = 8\,034\,627\,303\,276\,167 \tag{10}$$

$$PK[2,3] = 21\,377\,621\,450\,388\,194 \tag{11}$$

$$PK[2,4] = 7\,740\,397\,556\,851\,464 \tag{12}$$

$$PK[2,5] = 22\,229\,818\,744\,333\,528 \text{ and the sum is} \tag{13}$$

$$\text{Total} = 68\,295\,315\,332\,243\,594 \qquad . \tag{14}$$

This value calculated for C is sent as the encryption of the plaintext message 150.

3   Decryption

Decryption requires knowledge of the two secret keys, the prime p and the primitive root g. C is the sum of discrete logarithms. Since the inverse of a discrete logarithm is exponentiation, and since C is a sum of logarithms, the exponential of C must be a product. That product is

$$g^C \quad \bmod p \tag{15}$$

which, in the running example and making use of the Maple^{TM} software package, is found to be

$$12\,096\,214\,091\,399. \tag{16}$$

To find the original entries that came from the secret matrix M, factor this product

$$12\,096\,214\,091\,399 = (239)\,(263)\,(431)\,(521)\,(857). \tag{17}$$

These factors are found to be in the secret matrix M at the locations $[5,1]$, $[3,2]$, $[2,3]$, $[2,4]$, and $[2,5]$,

$$M = \begin{bmatrix} 797 & 887 & 683 & 307 & 541 & 353 \\ 761 & 379 & \mathbf{263} & \mathbf{431} & \mathbf{521} & 211 \\ 739 & \mathbf{239} & 811 & 367 & 907 & 167 \\ 719 & 743 & 419 & 557 & 503 & 701 \\ \mathbf{857} & 131 & 839 & 293 & 227 & 251 \\ 223 & 199 & 631 & 359 & 571 & 103 \end{bmatrix} . \tag{18}$$

Going now to the same locations in the preliminary matrix PM yields the addends of 150, and the plaintext P is revealed by summing these entries. These steps are summarized in Algorithm 4.

3.1   A Recapitulation of the Major Steps in the Algorithm

Here are the steps in the complete algorithm:

Algorithm 4: The decryption procedure

Data: Given the ciphertext Total
Result: The plaintext message P

Calculate the exponential of C and call it Exp. Exp $= g^C \bmod p$

1 Since Total is the sum of discrete logarithms to the base $g \bmod p$, its
  exponential must be a product of one or more integers.
  Calculate Exp $= g^C \bmod p$ to return this product.

Factor the product Exp

2 Calculate the factors of Exp. The factors of Exp are from the matrix M.

Determine the plaintext message

3 Determine the location of each of the factors of Exp in the matrix M. These
  locations must also be the locations of the addends of the plaintext message in
  the matrix PM. Using these locations, determine the corresponding addends.
  Sum these addends in order to reveal the plaintext P.

Setup

1. Decide the value of m for all the square $m \times m$ matrices PM, PK, and M to
   be created; thereby determining the number of possible messages n where

$$0 \leq \binom{2m-1}{m \quad 1} \leq n - 1. \tag{19}$$

2. Create the $m \times m$ preliminary matrix PM using the rotated Pascal Triangle.
3. Randomly choose m^2 unique primes and use them to randomly populate the
   $m \times m$ matrix M. Keep matrix M a secret.
4. Find a prime p whose number of digits d_{prime} is such that $d_{prime} > (m-1) \times d$
   where d is the number of digits in the largest prime in matrix M.
5. Find a primitive root g of p. Keep both p and g secret.
6. Build the public key matrix PK consisting of the logarithms to base $g \bmod$
   p of the prime entries in matrix M maintaining their ordering.

Encrypting

1. Use matrix PM to find the locations of the addends of the plaintext message P.
2. Use the locations found in the previous step and sum the entries in the public
   key matrix PK at these very same locations. The sum obtained, C, is the
   ciphertext.

Decrypting

1. Calculate the exponential Exp $= g^C \bmod p$.

2. Since the exponential found in the previous step is the product of primes found in matrix M, all that is needed is to find these primes and where they are located in the matrix M. An easy way to do this, without resorting to advanced factoring algorithms, is to use matrix M in the same way matrix PM was used originally to find the route for encrypting the plaintext. The factors, of course, are already in M. The method follows:-

3. Set $T = $ Exp and $plaintext = 0$.

4. Begin by checking the prime in the lower left corner of Matrix $M[m, 1]$. Check whether T mod $M[m, 1] = 0$. If true, then set $plaintext = A[m, 1]$ since $A[m, 1]$ is an addend of the plaintext. Also, since $M[m, 1]$ is a divisor of T, set $T = T/M[m, 1]$. Move one column to the right and then consider $M[m, 2]$ as a possible factor of T. Otherwise, ignore $M[m, 1]$ and move up by 1 row and now consider $M[m - 1, 1]$ as a possible factor of T. Each time, move up 1 row in matrix M whenever a factor of T is not found. Move to the right 1 column if a factor is found. This search method is exactly the same one used in finding the route from the Pascal Matrix PM used in encryption, except division is involved instead of subtraction. Whenever a factor of T is found, add the corresponding element of matrix PM at the same location in M where the factor was found to the current value of $plaintext$ and divide T by the new-found factor. Continue until all the factors of T are found.

5. When the last factor of T is found T will equal 1.

6. The final value of $plaintext$ will be the original message P.

4   Practical Issues

4.1   Determining the Size of Matrices PM, M, and PK

In explaining this algorithm, we have used a toy example involving 6×6 matrices. Since a 6×6 matrix can only accommodate 462 messages, it is far too small for practical purposes. It is also trivial to break. Since there are only 462 possible sums in the public-key matrix PK, all possible sums can be calculated, stored, and looked up when a ciphertext is observed.

To implement and test this algorithm, the authors used a 100×100 matrix with 10 000 entries. The programming language used was Maple^{TM}. A 100×100 matrix meant that the number of possible messages is

$$\binom{199}{99} = 45\,274\,257\,328\,051\,640\,582\,702\,088\,538\,742\,081\,937\,252\,294\,837\,706\,668\,420\,660 \quad (20)$$

a number consisting of 59 digits. Constructing the preliminary matrix PM is straightforward. However, creating the secret matrix M consisting of primes requires particular thought because the size of the primes affects the choice of p and the expected size of the discrete logarithms to be stored in the public-key matrix PK. The maximum number of addends in any plaintext integer is $m - 1$, where m is the number of rows, or columns, in the preliminary matrix PK. Call this number max. In our 100×100 test matrix, this could mean as many as 99 addend locations could be found for a given plaintext message. This requires that 99 entries will be needed from the public-key matrix PK to encipher the plaintext. Since adding discrete logarithms is the equivalent of multiplying their antilogarithms, the entries in the secret matrix M, the size of the entries in M is a significant parameter of the algorithm. If the entries in the secret matrix M are on the order of 6 digits each as they were in the test program created by the authors, a given plaintext message might have 99 addends. In this case, the actual product of the primes in M will have $6 \times max = 6 \times 99 = 594$ digits. Call this value $maxdigits$. This has ramifications.

4.2 Determining the Prime p and the Primitive Root g

The maximum product of the primes in M also determines a lower bound on the single large prime p needed to act as the modulus of the system in which the discrete logarithms will be calculated. The number of digits in p must be greater than $maxdigits$. Once p is known, it is necessary to calculate a primitive root g of p. The public-key matrix PK can now be created by finding the discrete logarithms to the base g mod p of the primes in M.

4.3 Overcoming Roadblocks in Calculating Discrete Logarithms

Working with a very large randomly chosen prime p, finding discrete logarithms in a reasonable time is usually impossible unless the prime p has special properties. Finding discrete logarithms can be much easier and more practical if the prime p is a prime such that $p - 1$ has small factors. To work with such primes, one can choose many small primes, including a power of 2, to make their product an even integer, multiply them together, add 1, and test the resulting odd integer for primality. In our test case, we chose sets of random primes less than 150 000 whose product would have greater than 594 digits and tested for primality. Maple™ had no difficulty in finding some. The Number Theory package with Maple™ has a function for calculating primitive roots. For the matrix M, we randomly chose 10 000 primes of 6 digits.

5 Security Considerations

One consideration is that *a change in one of the plaintext digits should significantly change the ciphertext*. This happens in this algorithm because the algorithm will choose different addends during encryption. For example, in the 6×6 toy example, changing the plaintext 150 whose addends are $\{126, 15, 4, 3, 2\}$ to 151 makes the new addends $\{126, 15, 10\}$ and forces a very different selection from the public matrix PK. This will produce a new total for the ciphertext produced. Another consideration is that *no pattern be discoverable in the published data for encryption*. An earlier paper that refers to the Pascal triangle approach had an attempt to hide the manner in which the addends are chosen from the preliminary matrix PM in the public-key matrix PK [2]. In the algorithm in this paper, finding the items chosen from the public-key matrix PK during decryption does not depend in any way on the structure of the Pascal Triangle used for matrix PM.

6   Cryptanalysis

This algorithm depends on determining discrete logarithms to populate the public-key matrix PK. Usually, in papers on the discrete logarithm problem, the issue involves determining the logarithms given the prime p and the primitive root g. Both of these values are kept secret in this algorithm. The public-key matrix PK is the only set of integers available for cryptanalysis. For any given integer X mod p with prime p whose logarithm Z where $Z = \log_g X$ mod p with a primitive root g, there are an infinity of primes and associated primitive roots which will have the same value for Z. As a simple example, given the primes $2\,029$ and $9\,929$ with primitive roots 2 and 10 and the integers 1129 and 7850 the two logarithms, $\log_2 1\,129 = 100$ mod $2\,029$ and $\log_{10} 7\,850 = 100$ mod $9\,929$, are both the same, namely 100. Finding the secret prime p and the secret primitive root g, knowing only the public matrix PK, when using a very large prime, would seem practically impossible.

In the RSA public-key system, the public modulus system is the product of two large primes, large enough to defeat their factorization. This algorithm uses factoring, but only after the ciphertext has been processed by exponentiation using the secret keys, the prime p, and the chosen primitive root g.

7   Attempts to Reproduce This Algorithm's Procedure for Generating the Secret Keys

Since the **method** of generating the secret keys, i.e., the prime p, the primitive root g, and the matrix M of primes, is public knowledge, one must determine if a cryptanalyst could determine the values for p, g, and M by applying the methods with random data until the secret keys appear given enough time. The answer is a definite *No!* The secret prime p is created by multiplying small primes together, multiplying by a power of 2, adding 1, and finally determining if the product is prime. Keeping the size of the primes small enables the processes of factorization and finding discrete logarithms to be manageable. The authors employed the method of using only randomly chosen primes less than 150 000. There are 13 848 primes less than 150 000. The authors then multiplied 130 of these primes together, multiplied by 2 to make the product even, and then tried multiplying by one more prime, adding 1, and checking for primality. On failing, the prime added was dropped, and another was chosen. This process was repeated until one was found. The prime found had 738 digits. There are many to find. There is a function $\psi(x, y)$ in analytic number theory for finding the number of integers greater than x which, when factored, have no prime factors $> y$. As an illustration of *many to find*, Sorenson showed that an approximation to this function for all $x \leq 2^{1\,000}$ with no factors $> 2^{20}$ is approximately $9.998e+204$ [3–5]. This says that, approximately, for all integers with less than 302 digits, about x of them, where x is an integer with about 90 digits, factor into primes that are less than $1\,048\,576$. Finally, finding a modular logarithm took less than 4 seconds. Of course, finding the modular logarithm of $10\,000$ primes will take several hours but only needs to be done once. If one hopes to repeat this process, the number of possible choices of 131 primes from $13\,500$ of them yields approximately 7.4×10^{318} different possibilities. Choosing $10\,000$ primes from this same set for the secret matrix M has even more possibilities, approximately $1.4 \times 10^{3\,353}$.

8 Application

The paper demonstrates a cryptographically strong public-key encryption system with the matrix dimension $m = 100$. This algorithm could be used in an application with a symmetric encryption algorithm. For this public-key algorithm to encrypt a symmetric 256 bit key, the matrix dimension needs to be increased to $m = 131$. The corresponding number of messages is

$$\binom{2m-1}{m-1} = \binom{261}{130}, \tag{21}$$

which is approximately 1.82×10^{77}. The matrix M now contains $m^2 = 17\,161$ prime numbers and each prime number still has up to 6 digits. The storage requirements for M are shown in the third column of Table 1; the second column for $m = 100$ is included for comparison. For $m = 131$, *max* is 130 and with 6 digits, the product, *maxdigits*, is 780. A prime number, p, where $p-1$ is smooth, was found with 816 digits. A primitive root, g, was found, having 815 digits. The public key matrix, PK now has $17\,161$ elements, in which each discrete logarithm has up to 816 digits; the storage requirement is shown in Table 1, where the net requirement to store the digits of the secret and public keys are shown to be $14\,107\,973$ digits. Converting the storage requirements from digits to Megabytes, respectively, for m equal to 100 and 131, gives approximately 3.09 Megabytes and 5.87 Megabytes.

Table 1. Storage requirements of the secret key, p, g, M, and public key, PK

Item	Storage in digits $m = 100$	Storage in digits $m = 131$
p	738	816
g	737	815
M	60 000	102 966
PK	7 380 000	14 003 376
Net	7 441 475	14 107 973

9 Conclusion

For the demonstrated example with a matrix dimension of 100, one is tempted to draw back when faced with a secret key consisting of 10 000 primes, each of 738 digits, or less, but that is approximately 3.09 Megabytes of storage, hardly a matter of overwhelming significance in this era. In time, the production of a general-purpose quantum computer may make the discrete logarithm problem and the factoring of large integers much more feasible without resorting to specially constructed primes, but finding one from a set that has more elements than atoms in the known observable universe, estimated to be between 10^{78} and 10^{82}, will be a daunting task.

References

1. Rubinstein-Salzedo, S.: Cryptography, Palo Alto, CA, USA. Springer, Cham (2018). https://doi.org/10.1007/978-3-319-94818-8
2. Cooper, R.H., Hunter-Duvar, R., Patterson, W.: A more efficient public-key cryptosystem using the pascal triangle. In: IEEE International Conference on Communications, World Prosperity Through Communications, Boston, MA, USA, vol. 3, pp. 1165–1169. IEEE (1989). https://doi.org/10.1109/ICC.1989.49866
3. Saias, E.: Sur le nombre des entiers sans grand facteur premier. J. Number Theory **32**(1), 78–99 (1989). https://doi.org/10.1016/0022-314X(89)90099-1
4. Sorenson, J.P.: A fast algorithm for approximately counting smooth numbers. In: Bosma, W. (ed.) ANTS 2000. LNCS, vol. 1838, pp. 539–549. Springer, Heidelberg (2000). https://doi.org/10.1007/10722028_36
5. Granville, A.: Smooth numbers: computational number theory and beyond. In: Buhler, J.P., Stevenhagen, P. (eds.) Algorithmic Number Theory: Lattices, Number Fields, Curves and Cryptography, New York, NY, USA, pp. 267–323. Cambridge University Press (2008). https://www.cambridge.org/9780521808545

Objects Detection in an Image by Color Features

Georgi Tsonkov[1]([✉]) and Magdalena Garvanova[2]

[1] Elektro Mechanik Sonnenschein GmbH, Bischofswiesen, Germany
gtsonkov@tsoftcomputers.de
[2] University of Library Studies and Information Technologies, Sofia, Bulgaria
m.garvanova@unibit.bg

Abstract. The present article introduces an algorithm for object detection in video material based on color characteristics. This algorithm demonstrates efficiency in conditions of varying illumination, low video resolution, as well as when dealing with a substantial number of objects of the same type, but with distinct color attributes. Its potential applications encompass tasks related to object retrieval through real-time video surveillance using stationary and mobile cameras, both in real-time scenarios and video recordings.

Keywords: Video analyser · Color filter · Object detection · Computer vision

1 Introduction

In the contemporary world of high technology, video processing and analysis are assuming increasingly significant roles across various domains. To meet this burgeoning interest, diverse software products have been developed, offering capabilities for various forms of video data analysis [1, 2]. Particularly noteworthy in today's context is the analysis of video content within the framework of security and safety. Modern software products feature an extensive array of algorithms and functions that greatly automate the process of video analysis [3, 4]. These algorithms enable object detection, facial recognition, motion analysis, and more. They provide the means to extract valuable information from video content, which can serve diverse purposes, including incident prevention, criminal investigation, business process optimization, enhanced user experience as well as monitoring of disasters [16]. Thus, the evolution of contemporary software solutions for video content analysis not only facilitates and enhances the work of individuals engaged in video data processing but also holds substantial potential to reshape how we interact with video materials and utilize the information encapsulated within them.

Among the various types of video analysis, such as object recognition [5], image focusing [6, 7], motion detection, and facial recognition [8], lies the possibility of object detection based on their color characteristics. Although object and facial recognition constitute pivotal aspects of video analysis, situations may arise where this task proves challenging or even unfeasible due to factors like low lighting, blurring, restricted viewing angles, privacy regulations that prohibit the storage and/or use of training data for algorithms without explicit consent from concerned individuals. In such scenarios, object

© The Author(s), under exclusive license to Springer Nature Switzerland AG 2023
B. Shishkov and A. Lazarov (Eds.): ICTRS 2023, CCIS 1990, pp. 65–76, 2023.
https://doi.org/10.1007/978-3-031-49263-1_5

and facial detection through color attributes emerges as an effective approach, with the potential to be exceptionally useful, especially in the absence of alternative information about the sought-after entities.

The present development will introduce software for color search within video content, where the color range can be defined by the user. This software solution employs filtering and searching for specific color ranges to detect and annotate areas within video content that correspond to desired color characteristics set by the user. This can be particularly useful for identifying objects with specific color attributes, such as vehicle colors, clothing colors, and more. In practice, this method yields excellent results, especially when searching within crowds, distant objects, or numerous objects dispersed across a wide area.

This algorithm and the integrated application can be used for both static video files and real-time image analysis or streaming. This versatility allows the application to be utilized in various fields. For instance, in the domain of video surveillance, object detection based on color characteristics can aid in locating vehicles with particular body colors in large parking lots or on roads, as well as identifying individuals with specific clothing colors amidst dense crowds (concerts, markets, or other bustling venues), across spacious areas amidst other objects, and beyond. Moreover, in the realm of medicine, color-based detection of specific characteristics can be employed for analyzing medical images or video material. For example, when studying skin conditions, certain color attributes could serve as indicators of potential pathological states. Notably, color detection can also prove valuable in the realm of computer graphics and visualization. When crafting virtual worlds and scenes, object detection based on color characteristics can simplify the process of placing markers on various elements, contributing to a more realistic visualization and animation.

2 Algorithm Description

As previously mentioned, both static video files and live video streams can serve as input data for the algorithm. Initially, each frame of the video is loaded into the computer's memory as a RGB object, representing a matrix containing every pixel of the captured image. In the subsequent step, a copy of the acquired frame is generated, on which the necessary filters for object detection and annotation will be applied. The user can specify the desired color range for the sought-after objects by defining the lower and upper boundaries of the target color spectrum. This is necessary because accurately determining the exact color of an object and how it will be captured by the video processor of individual recording devices can be challenging. The algorithm's operation is schematically presented in Fig. 1.

The color range is defined by the user through specifying a primary RGB color for the search. Once the color is determined, a value is set to represent the offset along the RGB scale from the primary color, thus creating the upper and lower boundaries of the desired color range.

Using the *EmguCV (OpenCV)* library [9], these parameters are passed to the method of the static class *CvInvoke.InRange()*, which determines which pixels of the input image fall within the specified color range or performs the so-called segmentation. Once segmented, the method in the static class *CvInvoke.FindContours()* traverses the identified

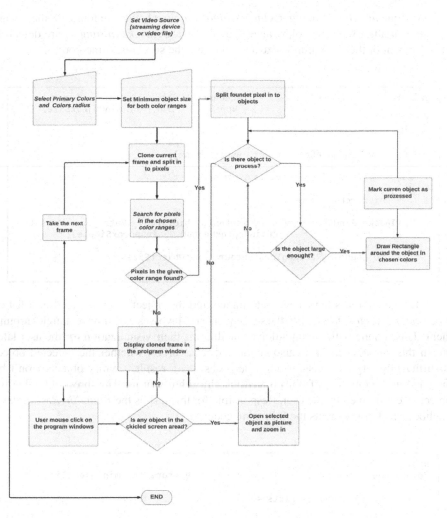

Fig. 1. Flowchart of the algorithm

regions and outlines their external contours, thereby grouping them into distinct objects. This operation can be succinctly summarized as follows:

1. A check is performed to identify areas of neighboring pixels with similar attributes, such as colors within the specified range.
2. For each of these areas (components), contours are calculated. In this algorithm, contours represent the outer boundaries of the areas. They consist of a sequence of points forming closed polygons or curves around the region.
3. The contours are added to a collection of vectors, with each component having its corresponding contour. This collection of vectors is stored in an object of type *VectorOfVectorOfPoint*.

Consequently, by utilizing *CvInvoke.FindContours()*, the contours of the image regions that align with the color range specified via *CvInvoke.InRange()* are detected. This segment of the algorithm is executed through the subsequent method:

```
private IEnumerable<Rectangle> TrackCurrentColor(IInputArray lower,
                         IInputArray upper, Mat rgb, int minObjectSize)
{
    Mat mask = new Mat();

    CvInvoke.InRange(rgb, lower, upper, mask);

    VectorOfVectorOfPoint contours = new VectorOfVectorOfPoint();

    Mat hierarchy = new Mat();

    CvInvoke.FindContours(mask, contours, hierarchy, RetrType.External,
                         ChainApproxMethod.ChainApproxSimple);

    return BoundingRectangles(contours, minObjectSize);
}
```

After the contours have been determined and the objects are collected in a list of type *VectorOfVectorOfPoint* [9], the subsequent step involves outlining rectangles around them. This is done with the intention of facilitating their visualization for the user later on. In this phase, a check is also conducted to ascertain whether the detected object is sufficiently large for visualization purposes. As a result, smaller objects won't be included in the final list of objects that the algorithm returns. The threshold value for object size is defined by the user. Responsible for this task is the *BoundingRectangles()* method, which implements the following code:

```
private IEnumerable<Rectangle>
BoundingRectangles(VectorOfVectorOfPoint vectors,int minObjectSize)
{
    HashSet<Rectangle> rects = new HashSet<Rectangle>();

    for (int i = 0; i < vectors.Size; i++)
    {
        Rectangle rect = CvInvoke.BoundingRectangle(vectors[i]);

        if ((rect.Width * rect.Height) >= minObjectSize)
        {
            rects.Add(rect);
        }
    }

    return rects;
}
```

Once the objects are marked with rectangles and other metadata such as coordinates on the frame, area, count, etc., are stored, they are superimposed onto the cloned frame. Using another function, the rectangles themselves are colored with a hue chosen by the user. This ensures their visibility to the user to whom the frame will be presented.

During the visualization on the user interface, the user is given the capability to select any of the marked objects using the left mouse button. For this purpose, the algorithm provides a method that tracks events from clicks on the user interface. If such an event is detected, the algorithm checks whether the click's coordinates correspond to those of the previously detected objects. If a match is found, the program extracts the respective segment from the original frame before cloning and presents it in a separate window as a static image. This window is displayed with dimensions and coordinates derived from the selected region on the cloned frame and can be zoomed in for detailed examination, allowing the user to scrutinize the chosen area meticulously.

3 Implementation

The algorithm for object detection by color features has been adapted as a foundation for the development of a software tool intended to facilitate the practical implementation of the algorithm in various applications. The program has been implemented using the C# programming language and the.Net Core platform [10].

After launching the software, the user can choose a source of video data, which can be a video transfer device (such as a camera or DVD player) or a video file. In the case of selecting a video transfer device, an additional algorithm checks the available modes of the device. Most devices offer modes with different resolutions and frame rates. This enables the user to select the most appropriate mode for their specific requirements. An example of such selection is illustrated in Fig. 2.

In the "Prozesseinstellungen" window (translated from German as "process settings"), the fundamental parameters required for the algorithm's functioning are localized. An illustration of this window is provided in Fig. 3. The program supports object detection in two distinct colors, with the user deciding whether to employ both colors or just one. Configuring the primary colors is accomplished through the buttons *Farbe 1 Einstellen* (Set Color 1) and *Farbe 2 Einstellen* (Set Color 2). After selecting the primary color using the *Radius* tool, which is available separately for both colors, the deviation from the primary color – or in other words, the color range within which the algorithm will search for objects – can be adjusted. Currently, the algorithm operates within the RGB color space [11], which, to some extent limits the choice of color range. An extension to the algorithm is under development, enabling support for other color models that offer more optimized color filtering and precise specification of color ranges for filters such as HSL and HSV models. Additionally, a trained Artificial Intelligence is also in development, which will be capable of recognizing objects. This will allow the algorithm not only to filter for desired colors but also to identify objects of that color (for example, exclusively red vehicles or individuals with specific clothing colors).

The "Min. Objekt Grösse" (Min. Object size) tool enables users to specify the minimum size of objects for detection associated with each of the primary colors. This ensures that the algorithm filters out objects that do not meet the specified size requirements. This simplifies the analysis process and facilitates subsequent video processing.

The software also offers options to adjust the color and thickness of the contours that outline the detected objects. This gives users the ability to select a contrasting color for outlining individual regions, making them more distinguishable during frame analysis.

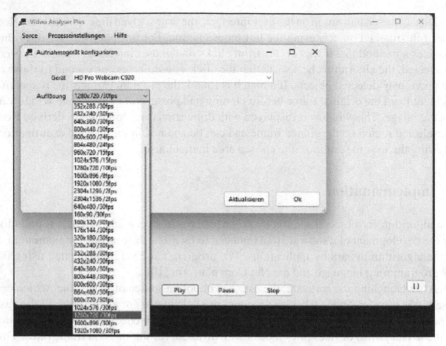

Fig. 2. Program main screen with device option

By activating the *Start Tracking* option for each of the primary colors, the algorithm becomes operational and begins processing video frames, filtering objects according to the established parameters.

Once the algorithm's parameters are set and a data source is chosen, pressing the *Play* button will initiate the playback of video data. The algorithm will analyze each frame based on the defined criteria and display the results in the program's main window. If objects are detected within the specified color range, they will be outlined in rectangles using the color chosen by the user.

Upon activating any of the rectangles using the mouse, the area outlined by it will be displayed as a static image in a new enlarged, additional window, as shown in Fig. 4.

This window can be zoomed in or out, automatically adjusting the size of the image within it. This provides a better opportunity for the user to analyze the selected object. For this purpose, an event has been implemented to track activity on the application's screen. If there is any activity, the coordinates of the user-selected point on the screen are captured, and then it is scaled to the original frame dimensions. This step is necessary in case the user has changed the screen size (e.g., selected the *Full Screen* option), ensuring that the algorithm will accurately return the activated object.

Following this, the objects are sorted by size, thus avoiding a scenario where the algorithm has detected two objects nested within each other, and upon requesting the smaller of the two, it would return both or only the larger one. The method responsible for this task takes the following form:

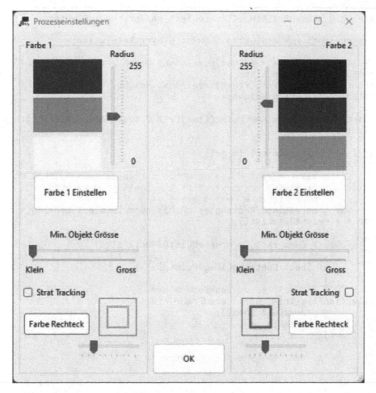

Fig. 3. Settings screen

Fig. 4. The selected object is displayed in a new window

```
private void screenBox_MouseClick(object sender, MouseEventArgs e)
{
    var currentSorceResolution = this._player.Resolution;

    float scaleFactorX = (float)screenBox1.Width /
currentSorceResolution.Width;
    float scaleFactorY = (float)screenBox1.Height /
currentSorceResolution.Height;

    Point imagePoint = new Point((int)(e.X / scaleFactorX), (int)(e.Y /
scaleFactorY));

    if (this.objectsColor1 != null)
    {
        //The list of rectangles shoud be sorted to assure, that when
user click on of those, to appier firs the smallest deteckted area
        //if there are some nested areas
        var orderedListOfRectangles = this.objectsColor1.OrderBy(x =>
x.Width * x.Height).ToList();

        foreach (var rect in orderedListOfRectangles)
        {
            if (rect.Contains(imagePoint))
            {
                ShowSelected zoomForm = new
ShowSelectionForm(this._unfilteredFrame, rect);
                zoomForm.Show();
                break;
            }
        }
    }
… //The same is done for the second color.
    }
```

When the software operates with stored video files like .avi, .mp4, or others, it provides additional functionalities for the user. These include the ability to accelerate or slow down playback and the presence of an integrated time-line. This integrated time-line allows for quick and convenient selection of a specific moment in the video that the user wishes to view.

During the operation of the program with real-time video streaming from an external source, these functionalities are not active. The reason is that during live streaming, the transmitted data is in real-time, and there is no possibility to rewind or change the playback speed, as the information has already been sent and is not locally stored by the program.

4   Results and Analysis

The application in which the algorithm for object search based on their color characteristics is integrated has already been provided for testing and gratuitous utilization by certain governmental agencies in Germany within the domain of security, public order maintenance, and rescue operations. Its primary objective is to provide support and facilitate their tasks.

To demonstrate the capabilities of the application, a recorded video was used, captured by a civil drone. The objective of this experiment was to employ the program to detect vehicles of a specific color that might be challenging to discern by the drone operator's naked eye. Additionally, a recording mode with relatively lower resolution was chosen to showcase the algorithm's maximum potential at the present stage. To preserve confidentiality and ensure the inviolability of personal space, frames without faces or identifiable license plates were selected.

The test scenario encompasses defined color ranges, as depicted in Fig. 5, with the objective of detecting vehicles exhibiting colors closely aligned with the specified ranges. Due to the inclusion of numerous environmental elements within the selected color range, such as wooded areas and portions of building facades, the option for filtering out the smallest objects during algorithm processing has been adopted. To enhance visibility, objects falling within the color range associated with color 1 will be enclosed by green rectangles, while those in color range 2 will be encompassed by pink rectangles.

During the video processing, as shown in Fig. 6, the algorithm identifies several objects in the two-color ranges. Upon closer inspection, it becomes apparent that one of these objects is a gray-green car, falling within the color range associated with color 2. When this object is activated by the user, the outlines of the car become clearly visible, situated right beneath a tree exhibiting hues reminiscent of the car's colors, as perceived by the human eye.

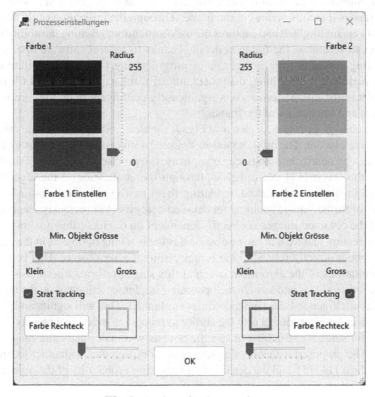

Fig. 5. Settings for the experiment

Fig. 6. Detecting objects

The diminished video quality and the object's similar colors to the surrounding environment render it inconspicuous in the frame. Through the utilization of the algorithm, this object gets highlighted and captures the user's attention, granting the ability to pause the video and scrutinize the frame in detail. Thanks to several software optimizations, incorporating concepts from asynchronous programming [12], the algorithm exhibits excellent performance, enabling the processing of a substantial number of frames per second. Naturally, this performance is significantly contingent upon the computational capabilities and the quality of the frames.

In the subsequent frame, depicted in Fig. 7, the detected vehicles in the other color range become evident. The drone's motion, coupled with certain external factors such as shadows cast by nearby buildings, can complicate the precise recognition of the targeted objects in the frame [13]. Nevertheless, through the application of the algorithm, the objects are identified and marked, rendering them easily discernible and offering the possibility of further image zooming for detailed analysis. As previously mentioned, the quality of the obtained images is directly dependent on the recording quality.

An interesting feature that can be observed is the marking of objects in the frame that may not appear directly related to the primary sought-after objects. This is due to the current limitations of the algorithm, which at this stage performs filtering solely based on color characteristics and size. In the upcoming implementation phase, the integration of artificial intelligence-based functionalities is planned. This will significantly enhance not only the color filtration but also the ability to recognize individual objects. Thus, the capability for selective searching of specific objects within defined color ranges will be achieved. The proposed detection algorithm can work together with other technologies and algorithms [14, 15], and the detection and tracking probability of the objects can be improved.

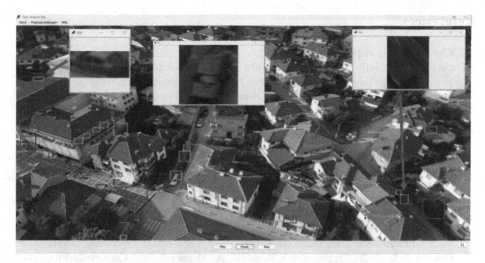

Fig. 7. Example of object detection in an urban environment

5 Conclusion and Future Work

In conclusion, object and face detection based on color characteristics provide an effective approach for analyzing and identifying objects in video materials when other methods such as object and face recognition may not always be efficiently applicable. When combined with the capability to recognize the types of objects themselves, this approach offers a distinct advantage, especially in conditions of varying illumination, capturing low-resolution images, or dealing with many objects of the same type but with different color characteristics.

Our future objective involves the integration of color-based methodologies with additional recognition algorithms, aiming to forge multifunctional systems that integrate the foremost contemporary techniques for detecting and analyzing objects within video content. This pursuit is projected to lead to a substantial enhancement in the precision of such systems.

This technique boasts a wide array of applications across various domains, ushering in novel prospects for automation and enhancement of the video analysis process. With the aid of a suitable and accessible interface in the form of a software application, the method becomes user-friendly and convenient to employ, even by individuals not versed in video processing.

Acknowledgement. This work was supported by the National Science Program "Security and Defense", which has received funding from the Ministry of Education and Science of the Republic of Bulgaria under the grant agreement № D01–74 /19.05.2022.

References

1. Kinovea (2023). https://www.kinovea.org/
2. Darfish (2023). https://sourceforge.net/software/product/Dartfish
3. Yuan, H.: Image target detection algorithm based on computer vision technology. In: 2022 International Conference on 3D Immersion, Interaction and Multi-sensory Experiences (ICDIIME), Madrid, Spain, pp. 10–13 (2022). https://doi.org/10.1109/ICDIIME56946.2022.00010
4. Li, Z., Jiang, D., Wang, H., Li, D.: Video image moving target recognition method based on generated countermeasure network. Comput. Intell. Neurosci. **2022**, 1–8 (2022). https://doi.org/10.1155/2022/7972845
5. Dange, V., et al.: Image processing and pattern recognition-based car classification for intelligent transportation system. In: 6th Smart Cities Symposium (SCS 2022), Hybrid Conference, Bahrain, pp. 271–275 (2022).https://doi.org/10.1049/icp.2023.0520
6. Garvanova, M., Ivanov, V.: Quality assessment of defocused image recovery algorithms. In: 3rd International Conference on Sensors, Signal and Image Processing – SSIP 2020, October 9–11, 2020, Prague, Czech Republic. ACM International Conference Proceeding Series, pp. 25–30. New York, NY, USA: ACM (2020). https://doi.org/10.1145/3441233.3441242
7. Garvanova, M., Ivanov, V.: Quality assessment of image deburring algorithms. IOP Conf. Ser.: Mater. Sci. Eng. **1031**(1), 1–5 (2021). https://doi.org/10.1088/1757-899X/1031/1/012051
8. Maria Dominic Savio, M., Deepa, T., Bonasu, A., Anurag, T.S.: Image processing for face recognition using HAAR, HOG, and SVM algorithms. J. Phys. Conf. Ser. **1964**(6), 062023 (2021). https://doi.org/10.1088/1742-6596/1964/6/062023
9. EmguCV Documentation (2023). https://www.emgu.com/wiki/index.php/Main_Page
10. ASP.NET Core Documentation (2023). https://learn.microsoft.com/de-de/aspnet/core/introduction-to-aspnet-core?view=aspnetcore-7.0
11. Pascal, D.: Areview of RGB Color Spaces – BabelColor, Monreal, Canada (2002)
12. Asynchron Programming C# (2022). https://learn.microsoft.com/de-de/dotnet/csharp/asynchronous-programming/async-scenarios
13. Garvanov, I., Garvanova, M., Ivanov, V., Lazarov, A., Borissova, D., Kostadinov, T.: Detection of unmanned aerial vehicles based on image processing. In: Shishkov, B., Lazarov, A. (eds.) Telecommunications and Remote Sensing: 11th International Conference, ICTRS 2022, Sofia, Bulgaria, November 21–22, 2022, Proceedings, pp. 37–50. Springer Nature Switzerland, Cham (2022). https://doi.org/10.1007/978-3-031-23226-8_3
14. Garvanov, I., Kabakchiev, C., Behar, V., Daskalov, P.: Air target detection with a GPS forward-scattering radar. In: XVIII International Symposium on Electrical Apparatus and Technologies – SIELA 2016, Bourgas, Bulgaria, pp. 1–4 (2016). https://doi.org/10.1109/SIELA.2016.7543000
15. Garvanov, I., Kabakchiev, C.: Radar detection and track determination with a transform analogous to the Hough transform. In: International Radar Symposium – IRS 2006, Krakow, Poland, pp. 121–124 (2006). https://doi.org/10.1109/IRS.2006.4338015
16. Shishkov, B., Verbraeck, A.: Making enterprise information systems resilient against disruptive events: a conceptual view. In: Shishkov, B. (ed.) BMSD 2020. LNBIP, vol. 391, pp. 38–54. Springer, Cham (2020). https://doi.org/10.1007/978-3-030-52306-0_3

Telecommunications and Remote Sensing: A Public Values Perspective

Boris Shishkov[1,2,3]($\boxtimes$) and Magdalena Garvanova[2]

[1] Institute of Mathematics and Informatics, Bulgarian Academy of Sciences, Sofia, Bulgaria
`b.b.shishkov@iicrest.org`
[2] Faculty of Information Sciences, University of Library Studies and Information Technologies, Sofia, Bulgaria
`m.garvanova@unibit.bg`
[3] Institute IICREST, Sofia, Bulgaria

Abstract. The impact of current telecommunications on life in developed countries is amazing, allowing for fast transmission of data over the Internet. This can also be usefully supported by sensor technologies, to allow for powerful remote sensing capabilities. As a result, huge amounts of data is showering us every second, inspiring in turn the developments in the area of data analytics where OLAP technologies allow for data extraction and fusion, for the sake of deriving really useful knowledge. Hence, ICT (Information and Communication Technology) is changing many aspects of our lives, making it possible to derive, transmit, and immediately use data on a global scale. This leads to the question: Has ICT improved our lives? Many answers to this question would be positive because the wide availability of useful data can facilitate many Human activities, no doubt about this. Nevertheless, this same data showering can also put at risk essential public values, such as safety, privacy, accountability, and trust. This paper analyzes the potential tensions between capabilities related to telecommunications and remote sensing, on one hand and such values, on the other hand, resulting in the definition of a corresponding conceptual model. Using it, we outline solution directions assuming a value-sensitive design over the developments of telecommunications/remote sensing systems. We provide illustrations accordingly, using several toy examples. Further research focuses on reflecting those conceptualizations in concrete design patterns (building blocks) that could usefully support the development of value sensitive ICT systems.

Keywords: Telecommunications · Remote sensing · Public values

1 Introduction

A number of new technologies have appeared, each one targeting specific aspects of large-scale distributed data-processing, that allow for handling very large data volumes with little financial cost [1]. Currently, it is also possible to transmit such data volumes, counting on advanced telecommunications at affordable cost [2]. Finally, sensing technology has developed in parallel, opening up new horizons for remote sensing [3, 4]. This

© The Author(s), under exclusive license to Springer Nature Switzerland AG 2023
B. Shishkov and A. Lazarov (Eds.): ICTRS 2023, CCIS 1990, pp. 77–89, 2023.
https://doi.org/10.1007/978-3-031-49263-1_6

all has given an interdisciplinary boost as it concerns the development of context-aware ICT (Information and Communication Technology) systems [6–16]. They are capable of providing the "right" piece of data, at the "right" time, in the "right" situation, for the sake of delivering effective situation-specific services, for the benefit of the service users and/or the environment. Hence, ICT is changing many aspects of our lives, making it possible to derive, transmit, and immediately use data on a global scale, aligned to the situation at hand.

In this regard, the important question "Has ICT improved our lives?" is simple to answer in general: YES, servicing of users is becoming more effective and situation-specific, and this is for sure useful and positive. Nevertheless, we argue that the "other side of the coin" concerns public values, such as safety, privacy, accountability, and trust [17] – are they put at risk with all abovementioned technical and technological developments? As it concerns SAFETY, can we always guarantee that localization would not put at risk a stakeholder, for example: a border security officer who may become a target for trespassers/smugglers? As it concerns PRIVACY, can we guarantee that upon gathering situation-specific data concerning the service user, privacy-sensitive details would not "leak out"? As it concerns ACCOUNTABILITY, can we guarantee accountability in cases where multiple stakeholders and technical systems are contributing to the service delivery, for example when services are delivered by drones that are often driven by several technical systems (the drone hardware/software, the ground hardware/software, and so on) and several stakeholders (the mission "owner", the controlling institutions, and so on)? As it concerns TRUST, can we guarantee adequate cooperation of users and stakeholders, that in turn requires minimal levels of trust in the system and/or in the relevant institutions? We observe that to date those issues are not covered exhaustively.

The limited coverage of public values in this regard is becoming a concern in our view, firstly with the growing pervasion of hardware and software into our lives, secondly with the broad global availability of large data volumes, and thirdly with the increased complexity of human-machine interaction [18–20].

Hence, we have a problem when multiple stakeholders interact, using data provided by multiple sources [23], with no powerful mechanisms to "control" the data and its usage. Most technical systems have been designed with an essential focus on service effectiveness with insufficient attention on public values [21, 22]. From other perspectives, however, "controlling" data and its usage may be dangerous by itself. And in the end, there may be tensions among different public values, requiring synchronization. We argue that the use of telecommunications and data technologies should be aligned with the adequate consideration of relevant public values. This implies that the way current ICT systems are implemented should be improved, by accommodating VALUE-SENSITIVE DESIGN [17, 21].

Addressing the above challenges is considered of huge relevance, especially in the light of ICT systems' increasing complexity (concerning telecommunications, remote sensing, and data) and societal pervasiveness, seen from examples such as autonomous cars and drone technology [18, 22, 28–31]. Here we see an explicit necessity of considering public values. The focus of this paper is mainly on the values conceptualization, rather than on the technology itself. Still, we analyze the potential tensions between capabilities related to telecommunications and remote sensing, on one hand and such values, on the other hand.

The contribution of the paper is therefore two-fold: The value-related tensions analysis (see above), resulting in the definition of a corresponding conceptual model; Using the model, we provide solution directions assuming a value-sensitive design over the developments of telecommunications/remote sensing systems.

The remainder of this paper is structured as follows: A thorough state-of-the-art analysis on public values related to telecommunications and remote sensing follows in Sect. 2. We present our proposed conceptual model in Sect. 3 and propose solution directions accordingly. In Sect. 4 we provide illustrations accordingly, using several toy examples. Finally, Sect. 5 provides the conclusions, discussing the contribution of the paper.

2 Background

In the current section, we firstly refer to related work, touching upon several key sources that are inspiring our work and have important influence in the area in general. Secondly, we outline our previous work that is relevant to the current contribution. Finally, we provide several useful conceptualizations that are inspired by the above.

2.1 Related Work

In analyzing related work, we firstly address public values, such as safety, privacy, accountability, and so on. Secondly, we address trust. That is because, we consider trust as crosscutting in the sense that no matter what public values are being addressed, their actual implementation would essentially depend on how much the user and/or stakeholders trust the system.

In our view, with regard to public values, the Washington influence is essential, especially the works of Batya Friedman who has key contribution to coining still in 1996 the notion of "Value-Sensitive Design" (VSD) [21]. According to the VSD philosophy, when designing technical systems, one should address not only the key user requirements, aiming at effectiveness in fulfilling user needs, but also the explicit and implicit concerns of relevant third parties, and the Society as a whole – this relates to current works in Sociotechnical Information Systems [24]. This all has inspired prominent works in Europe and mostly in The Netherlands where the research of Jeroen van den Hoven has brought together conceptual engineering and ethics in concert with VSD [17].

As it concerns trust, acknowledging many relevant aspects that can be considered (organizational aspects, technical aspects, legal aspects, and so on), we opt for addressing in particular policy-based trust and reputation-based trust as two main pillars for many current systems [25]. It is claimed that most often, one would trust anything either because of trusted related institutions or because of the evaluation (rating) of others.

Hence, key current challenges in this regard are:

- Incorporating VSD in the development of technical systems;
- Resolving possible tensions among different public values (imagine that it is challenging to fulfill safety and privacy at the same time);
- Aligning all this with corresponding trust considerations.

2.2 Our Previous Work

In our previous work, we have mainly considered VSD in relation to the challenge of developing Context-Aware (CA) information systems [6–16]. CA solutions have been firstly implemented around 20 years ago today when in areas, such as Tele-Medicine, a supportive technical system would have to adapt its "behavior" to the situation of the user (for example: a distantly monitored person) [5]. A contribution of ours in this regard is that in 2018 we have posed the claim that with regard to context-aware systems: some optimize system-internal processes, based on the context state at hand; others maximize the user-perceived effectiveness of delivered services, by providing different service variants depending on the situation of the user; still others are about offering value-sensitivity when the society demands so – this inspiring the identification of three categories of CA systems [26]. In addition, we have identified four enterprise modeling perspectives, namely language acts, regulations, public values, and energy – each of them claimed to be a theory/paradigm on its own [27]. In this way, we have not only made the consideration of public values explicit but we have also emphasized the importance of incorporating VSD in the overall system development process, considering values in synch with system effectiveness, internal optimizations, and so on. Finally, we have studied particular applicabilities related to drone technology: (i) In [22], we have addressed accountability-related concerns with regard to drones, considering in particular land border missions; (ii) In [28], we have addressed the societal impacts of drones, from a public values perspective, proposing mitigations-related views concerning possible value violations; this has also covered a balancing between design-time concerns and real-time concerns. All this previous work of ours is claimed to have further reinforced the views on explicitly considering public values and incorporating VSD in the development process accordingly. As it concerns trust, in [6], we have proposed ways of incorporating trust in CA services.

2.3 Conceptualizations

In the current sub-section, we firstly consider public values and secondly - trust.

Not claiming exhaustiveness, we only address three public values, namely: safety, privacy, and accountability, considered (in our view) of key importance and widely usable, see Fig. 1.

As the Figure suggests, those public values are not to be considered in isolation because there are potential tensions among them as follows:

- Often, guaranteeing the safety of the user and/or stakeholders assumes counting on privacy-sensitive data that is to be derived and used accordingly;
- Sometimes, resolving privacy-related issues, by anonymization (for example), may pose accountability-related challenges because the search for who is responsible for what may be hampered by prior privacy-driven data manipulations;
- Finally, it is possible that "heavy" systems burdened by accountability/traceability -related requirements, are slow and/or insufficiently effective in covering some safety-related demands.

Below, we discuss each of those public values in more detail.

Fig. 1. Considered public values

In our view SAFETY is mostly about culture, as suggested by Fig. 2, since damaging somebody or something is often a matter of perception. Imagine that a skyscraper is being built – in one country it may be acceptable that some persons die in accidents while in another country, it would be a "disaster" if even one person gets injured. Hence, if damaging issues are perceived differently, then also safety requirements would differ.

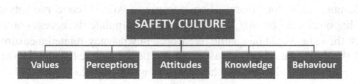

Fig. 2. Considering safety

Further, composition-wise, we project the safety notion as follows:

- The first "ingredient" are values – safety is about protecting somebody/something against some damages and the choice what to protect from concerns values: for example, designing an autonomous car may reflect demands to protect the user (the car driver) and/or possible third parties (pedestrians or cyclists) and/or the environment, and so on, and all those requirements may be conflicting with regard to each other [18]. It is important to make such prioritizations that properly reflect the underlying values. Sometimes being posh may be so important that even safety is partially compromised – very fast cars are an example of that.
- Safety is often a matter of perception and awareness – feeling safe (especially from the user perspective) is not only about the actual protection provided by the system but is also about the user's awareness and understanding that (s)he is being services in a way guaranteeing safety. For example, driving a car that is not perceived as safe, may result in burdening the driver with extra tension and stress that in turn may lead to accidents.
- Safety is also about attitudes – imagine that the owners of a company would mostly lean towards caring about the top management and not so much about the other

employees; this would result in high safety standards as it concerns the former and lower standards as it concerns the latter.

- Safety relates as well to knowledge because not knowing that something is dangerous would lead to no safety measures accordingly.
- Finally, safety is about behavior – different behavior patterns assume different risks and this in turn would lead to different safety measures. For example, the safety measures would be more relaxed about in-town cars (assuming a 50 km/h speed restriction) compared to cases that concern racing vehicles.

PRIVACY in turn is about control, risks, threats, security, and protection, as suggested by Fig. 3:

Fig. 3. Considering privacy

- Essentially, one could only enforce privacy-sensitive servicing, if (s)he has control over relevant system components. For example, if Alice is concerned about the privacy of her customers but she has no rights to manipulate the access control system modules, then she would be unable to enforce any privacy-related measures.
- Further, we claim that privacy measures are to be preventive (as opposed to reactive) because once somebody's privacy has been compromised, then it would be too "late" for anything. And if privacy is preventive, then anything concerning it should be about estimating risks rather than evaluating historical data. For example: if the private phone number of a prime minister is put on the institutional website, there is a very high risk of this leading to misuses even though it is not for sure that this would happen.
- Related to the above, privacy is about threats – acting upon all details would often be practically impossible and for this reason, privacy-related measures are to be directed only to (system) modules that concern potential threats. For example: threats of misuses concerning personal details are much higher in social media compared to a taxi-internal communication platform.
- Security is also a crucial "ingredient" here because privacy measures can only be adequate and effective if the system has proper security protection. For example, one may "hide" privacy-sensitive details of customers but if somebody else would "hack" the system, then (s)he would de facto get this information.
- And in the end, privacy is about protection because any privacy-related measures should be followed by corresponding protection measures – this would mean that the privacy measures have been actually implemented.

Finally, ACCOUNTABILITY is about the value of keeping the right stakeholder(s) responsible in case of failures/damages caused by the system – see Fig. 4. Composition-wise, we project the safety notion as follows:

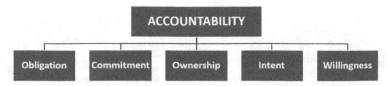

Fig. 4. Considering accountability

- In our view, the bottom line is that accountability is essentially bound to corresponding obligations because it would be inadequate keeping somebody accountable for things going beyond his or her obligations. For example: if a driver of an autonomous car has turned to "manual regime" and afterwards the car has caused an accident, then it wouldn't be appropriate keeping accountable the autonomous-driving-module producers.
- Accountability is about commitments as well because obligations would have limited value if not coupled to corresponding stakeholder commitments. Imagine that Brian is fulfilling the role "Bus Driver" and among the obligations of drivers in the company is property (bus) protection; nevertheless, Brian has stepped-in accidentally for several days because of absence of the regular bus driver and for this reason, Brian has not signed an employee contract; hence, Brian has not explicitly committed to all corresponding obligations and can only be kept accountable for things that concern the general traffic regulations, such as causing an accident, not observing the speed limit, and so on.
- We argue that ownership is always important and the "Big Boss" (or "Owner") is to be kept accountable in any cases concerning his or her business (of course, others may be kept accountable as well). That is because the "Owner" is "creating" the overall environment in which processes are happening and this should include key performance/failure indicators and other indicators that should raise alarm if anything is not right.
- Intents are also relevant because it is one thing if somebody has caused damages accidentally or if (s)he has done this intentionally; in both cases, the person should be kept accountable but we should be able to distinguish between the two, for the sake of treating stakeholders in a fair way.
- And in the end, willingness is to be taken into account – imagine that an employee is doing something against his or her will, just because the company Boss has ordered this; those things are to be carefully judged when considering accountabilities.

And in the end, we turn to TRUST, and particularly to policy-based trust vs. reputation-based trust – see above; in this we refer to [6]: As it concerns *policy-based trust*, access to information/services is regulated via some technical means; hence, this leads to *trust* by restricting the access to information to particular (groups of) users (for example: the use of *authentication mechanisms* such as passwords or digital signatures). The result of *policy-based trust* is the issuance of a permission to access a resource or the denial of that access. For conceptualizing this relationship, we can describe two *entities* (E_1 & E_2) that have access to a *resource* via a common *policy*. The *trusted space* is thus defined through this policy that is the same for all entities, see Fig. 5 – left.

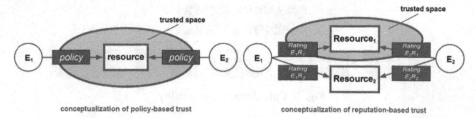

Fig. 5. Policy-based trust vs reputation-based trust (Source: [6], p. 98 ©2023, Springer, reprinted with permission)

Further, we consider *reputation-based trust* - here, the level of *trust* into a resource is calculated based on some kind of *reputation* assigned by other entities (for example: *rating systems* for resources such as websites, documents, or products - either *explicitly* (via ratings by users) or *implicitly* (via references). The result of *reputation-based trust* is thus not a binary decision but rather a gradual description of how much *trust* can be placed in some resource, see Fig. 5 - right. This can be conceptualized as follows: Two *entities* E_1 and E_2 which access *resources* R_1 and R_2 each conduct a *rating* of each *resource*, i.e. Rating E_1R_1 indicates that entity E_1 has rated resource R_1 with some numerical value. The combination of all ratings for a resource R_i from all entities E_i then defines the *trusted space*. The combination of the ratings may either be defined *centrally*, e.g. by the provider of the resource, or in a *decentralized fashion*, i.e. by each entity.

3 Proposal

Inspired by the above, we are considering a CA conceptual model that we have proposed in 2021 [7] (see Fig. 1 on p. 122) and we reflect this model in a conceptualization that is tailored to VSD – see Fig. 6.

As the Figure suggests:

- One or more entities may be in a SITUATION;
- We consider three types of entities, namely: USER, STAKEHOLDER, and SOCIETY;

And they have corresponding NEEDS;

- There are one or more IMPACTS concerning a SITUATION, that are partitioned as follows: USER IMPACTS, STAKEHOLDER IMPACTS, and SOCIETAL IMPACTS;
- A SERVICE PROVIDER should be capable of sensing such impacts;
- Needs are to be REFINED because often there would be TENSIONS among user needs, stakeholder needs, and Societal needs; a complex analysis is needed in this regard, establishing whose needs should PREVAIL – traditionally, the user needs are to be dominant but according to VSD, all needs should be super-imposed to each other for the sake of BALANCING interests and potential damages; then the goal should be fulfilling the user needs but only under the CONDITION that no damages are caused

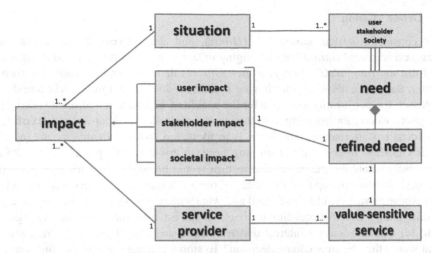

Fig. 6. Proposed conceptual model

to other stakeholders and/or Society (but still not compromising ESSENTIAL goals, such as life protection), for example: a primary user goal concerning an autonomous-car trip may be to reach the destination point as fast as possible but not at the price of causing an accident.

- Then a VALUE-SENSITIVE SERVICE is fulfilling a corresponding refined need.
- The SERVICE PROVIDER should be capable of delivering one or more such services in synch with the sensed impact (that in turn corresponds to the refined need mentioned above).
- That is how a SERVICE PROVIDER would be SERVICING relevant ENTITIES in a VALUE-SENSITIVE way.

Referring to the proposed conceptual model, we suggest several solution directions, as follows:

- User needs, stakeholder needs, and Societal needs should be super-imposed to each other for the sake of DERIVING REFINED NEEDS that are essentially driven by the user needs but are at the same time restricted by what could potentially damage other stakeholders and/or Society (still not compromising ESSENTIAL goals, such as life protection);
- Situational analyses are needed for the sake of identifying potential IMPACTS that concern the user, stakeholders, and the Society as a whole, such that those impacts are aligned to corresponding needs.
- Being within a situation, the service provider should be capable of sensing those impacts and delivering VALUE-SENSITIVE SERVICES accordingly, aligned to the refined needs.

4 Exemplification

The current section presents several toy examples that partially illustrate our VSD-related conceptualization and are directed towards telecommunications and remote sensing.

4.1 Drone Mission

Let's consider a system called "**D**" (*Drone*), and also **Alice**, **John**, **Sara**, and **Richard** who are "*entities*" not belonging to **D**. Imagine that **Alice** and **John** each can fulfil the *role* "**BPO**" (*Border Police Officer*) that concerns the *role type* **user**. Further, **Sara** is a news reporter having nothing to do with **D**. Finally, **Richard** is a trespasser. **D** is performing a mission for the benefit of **Alice** and **John** who need real-time photo/video data reflecting the situation at a controlled land border area. **Richard** is in focus but after some time **Sara** is in focus too. What does this mean? (a) The USER GOAL is to keep on transmitting because this would help **Alice** and **John** to precisely locate the trespasser that in turn would mean fulfilling the user goal; (b) This nevertheless goes against the needs of other relevant stakeholders – **Sara** in this case, whose privacy would be violated and what's more: she may even become a target for smuggling gangs if succeeding to "hack" **D** and establish that **Sara** is investigating them; (c) It is in Society's interest that **Richard** and other trespassers are arrested. What would then be an adequate decision? To stop the drone mission and find ways to instruct **Sara** to leave the area, before resuming the mission again. That is because even though the mission is fulfilling the user goal and is in Society's interest, it is potentially damaging as it concerns relevant stakeholders, **Sara** in this case.

4.2 Tele-Monitoring

Imagine that Steven being health-tele-monitored is in a confidential meeting with another person (Suzan). This is indicated by Steven and the System "knows" that the privacy of the other person should be guaranteed. But in case of worrying vital-sign readings received by the System, the System should identify nearby persons and establish contact with them, for asking help accordingly. Then should the System "reveal" Suzan? Yes, because:

• The user need is tele-monitoring and adequate care but then the needs of relevant stakeholders (in this case – Suzan and her privacy protection) would be hurt;
• Still, servicing the user should prevail because the situation is life-threatening for Steven and for this reason, hurting Suzan's needs would be justified (because they are not life-threatening with regard to her).

4.3 Cargo Transport

Let's consider an autonomous cargo car with Vaughan being the current user, in the sense that his parcel is to reach a destination point. Hence the user need is that the parcel reaches that point as fast as possible. The needs of relevant stakeholders (in this case – pedestrians appearing on the way of the car) concern safety – the pedestrians need to avoid any accident risks with regard to the autonomous car. Finally, the general societal needs concern regulations in the sense that the autonomous car (as well as all other vehicles in the city) respect the speed limit and other restrictions. Hence, the user goal (that does not concern life-threatening situations) is to be just partially fulfilled, sticking to imposed restrictions concerning the stakeholder and societal needs (see above); moreover, those needs concern potential life-threatening situations. Thus, the autonomous car would deliver the parcel but driving as fast as the speed limits and pedestrian safety allow.

5   Conclusions

This paper has considered value-sensitive design and its relevance as it concerns the development of ICT systems, particularly addressing the areas of telecommunications and remote sensing. We have conceptualized a value-sensitive servicing based on refined needs derived from user needs, stakeholder needs, and societal needs, balanced accordingly. The contribution of the paper is considered to be as follows: (i) We have explicitly considered value-sensitive design with regard to the development of ICT systems – this proves to be particularly relevant for the abovementioned areas while at the same time most such developments are not adequately considering public values, such as safety, privacy, and accountability (as well as the crosscutting notion of trust). (ii) We have proposed a conceptual model that is expected to be useful for both analysts and developers. (iii) We have proposed solution directions in addition to the conceptual model.

We have provided partial exemplification, by considering three toy examples.

In future research, we plan to: (a) Consider a larger example and use it to fully validate our proposed conceptual model; (b) Reflect it in concrete design patterns (building blocks) that could usefully support the development of value-sensitive ICT systems in the areas of telecommunications and remote sensing.

Acknowledgement. This work was supported by the National Science Program "Security and Defense", which has received funding from the Ministry of Education and Science of the Republic of Bulgaria under the grant agreement № D01–74 /19.05.2022.

References

1. Suthakar, U., Magnoni, L., Smith, D.R., et al.: An efficient strategy for the collection and storage of large volumes of data for computation. J. Big Data **3**, 21 (2016)
2. Shishkov, B., Lazarov, A. (Eds.) Telecommunications and Remote Sensing. Proceedings of the 11th International Conference, ICTRS 2022, Sofia, Bulgaria, November 21–22, 2022. Communications in Computer and Information Science, vol. 1730. Springer, Cham (2022). https://doi.org/10.1007/978-3-031-23226-8
3. Sensor.Community: Sensor Community (2023). https://sensor.community/en
4. Shishkov, B., Mitrakos, D.: Towards context-aware border security control. In BMSD'16, 6th International Symposium on Business Modeling and Software Design. SCITEPRESS (2016)
5. Wegdam M.: AWARENESS: A Project on Context AWARE Mobile NEtworks and ServiceS. In: Proceedings of 14th Mobile & Wireless Communications Summit. EURASIP (2005)
6. Shishkov, B., Fill, H.-G., Ivanova, K., van Sinderen, M., Verbraeck, A.: Incorporating trust into context-aware services. In: Shishkov, B. (ed.) Business Modeling and Software Design: 13th International Symposium, BMSD 2023, Utrecht, The Netherlands, July 3–5, 2023, Proceedings, pp. 92–109. Springer Nature Switzerland, Cham (2023). https://doi.org/10.1007/978-3-031-36757-1_6
7. Shishkov, B., van Sinderen, M.: Towards well-founded and richer context-awareness conceptual models. In: Shishkov, B. (ed.) BMSD 2021. LNBIP, vol. 422, pp. 118–132. Springer, Cham (2021). https://doi.org/10.1007/978-3-030-79976-2_7
8. Weiser M.: The Computer for the 21st Century. SIGMOBILE Mob. Comput. Commun. Rev. 3, 3 (July 1999), 3–11. ACM, New York, NY, USA (1999)

9. Dey, A., Abowd, G., Salber, D.: A conceptual framework and a toolkit for supporting the rapid prototyping of context-aware applications. Hum.-Comput. Interact. **16**, 2 (December) (2001)

10. Shishkov, B., van Sinderen, M.: On the context-aware servicing of user needs: extracting and managing context information supported by rules and predictions. In: Shishkov, B. (eds) Business Modeling and Software Design. BMSD 2022. Lecture Notes in Business Information Processing, vol 453. Springer, Cham (2022) https://doi.org/10.1007/978-3-031-11510-3_15

11. Dey, A.K., Newberger, A.: Support for context-aware intelligibility and control. In: Proceedings of SIGCHI Conference on Human Factors in Comp. Systems. ACM, USA (2009)

12. Bosems, S., van Sinderen, M., et al.: Models in the design of context-aware well-being applications. In: Meersman, R. (ed.) OTM 2014. LNCS, vol. 8842, pp. 37–42. Springer, Heidelberg (2014). https://doi.org/10.1007/978-3-662-45550-0_6

13. Alegre, U., Augusto, J.C., Clark, T.: Engineering context-aware systems and applications. J. Syst. Softw. **117**, C (July) (2016)

14. Alférez, G.H., Pelechano, V.: Context-aware autonomous web services in software product lines. In: Proceedings of 15th International SPLC Conference IEEE, CA, USA (2011)

15. Abeywickrama, D.B., Ramakrishnan, S.: Context-aware services engineering: models, transformations, and verification. ACM Trans. Internet Technol. J. **11**(3), Article 10. ACM (2012)

16. Shishkov B.: Designing Enterprise Information Systems, Merging Enterprise Modeling and Software Specification. Springer, Cham (2020) https://doi.org/10.1007/978-3-030-22441-7

17. Veluwenkamp, H., van den Hoven, J.: Design for values and conceptual engineering. Ethics Inf. Technol. **25**, 2 (2023). https://doi.org/10.1007/s10676-022-09675-6

18. Bartneck, C., Lütge, C., Wagner, A., Welsh, S.: Autonomous vehicles. In: An Introduction to Ethics in Robotics and AI. SpringerBriefs in Ethics. Springer, Cham (2021). https://doi.org/10.1007/978-3-030-51110-4_10

19. Fotohi, R., Abdan, M., Ghasemi, S.: A self-adaptive intrusion detection system for securing UAV-to-UAV communications based on the human immune system in UAV networks. J. Grid Comput. **20**, 22 (2022). https://doi.org/10.1007/s10723-022-09614-1

20. Hernigou, P., Lustig, S., Caton, J.: Artificial intelligence and robots like us (surgeons) for people like you (patients): toward a new human–robot-surgery shared experience. What is the moral and legal status of robots and surgeons in the operating room? Int. Orthop. **47**(2), 289 294 (2023). https://doi.org/10.1007/s00264-023-05690-4

21. Friedman, B.: Value-sensitive design. Interactions **3**(6), 16–23 (1996). https://doi.org/10.1145/242485.242493

22. Shishkov, B., Hristozov, S., Janssen, M., van den Hoven, J.: Drones in land border missions: benefits and accountability concerns. In: Proceedings of the 6th International Conference on Telecommunications and Remote Sensing (ICTRS'17). Association for Computing Machinery, New York, NY, USA, 77–86 (2017)

23. Han, J., Kamber, M., Pei, J.: Data Mining: Concepts and Techniques, 3rd edn. Morgan Kaufmann Publ. Inc., San Francisco, CA, USA (2011)

24. Barry, P., Doskey, S.: A sociotechnical approach to project success for multi-stakeholder, dynamic system development project environments. In: IEEE International Systems Conference (SysCon), Montreal, QC, Canada, pp. 1-7 (2020)

25. Bonatti, P., Duma, C., Olmedilla, D., Shahmehri, N.: An integration of reputation-based and policy-based trust management. Networks **2**(14), 10 (2007)

26. Shishkov, B., Larsen, J.B., Warnier, M., Janssen, M.: Three categories of context-aware systems. In: Shishkov, B. (ed.) Business Modeling and Software Design, pp. 185–202. Springer International Publishing, Cham (2018). https://doi.org/10.1007/978-3-319-94214-8_12

27. Shishkov, B., Bogomilova, A., Garvanova, M.: Four enterprise modeling perspectives and impact on enterprise information systems. In: Rocha, Á., Adeli, H., Reis, L.P., Costanzo, S., Orovic, I., Moreira, F. (eds.) WorldCIST 2020. AISC, vol. 1159, pp. 660–677. Springer, Cham (2020). https://doi.org/10.1007/978-3-030-45688-7_66

28. Shishkov, B., Garvanova, M.: The societal impacts of drones: a public values perspective. In: Shishkov, B., Lazarov, A. (eds) Telecommunications and Remote Sensing. ICTRS 2022. Communications in Computer and Information Science, vol. 1730. Springer, Cham https://doi.org/10.1007/978-3-031-23226-8_5

29. Dung, N.D., Rohacs, J.: The drone-following models in smart cities. In: 59th IEEE International Scientific Conference on Power and Electrical Engineering of Riga Technical University (RTUCON), Riga, Latvia, pp. 1–6 (2018)

30. Doran, H.D., Reif, M., Oehler, M., Stöhr, C., Capone, P.: Conceptual design of human-drone communication in collaborative environments. In: 50th Annual IEEE/IFIP International Conference on Dependable Systems and Networks Workshops (DSN-W), Valencia, Spain, pp. 118–121 (2020)

31. Besada, J.A., Bernardos, A.M., Bergesio, L., Vaquero, D., Campaña, I., Casar, J.R.: Drones-as-a-Service: a management architecture to provide mission planning, resource brokerage and operation support for fleets of drones. International IEEE Conference on Pervasive Computing and Communications Workshops (PerCom Workshops), Kyoto, Japan, pp. 931–936 (2019)

Integrated Platform for Vehicle Charging Based on Renewable Energy Resources

Radostin Dolchinkov(✉), Atanas Yovkov, Velizar Todorov, and Kristian Ventsislavov

Faculty of Computer Science and Engineering, Burgas Free University, Burgas, Bulgaria
rado@bfu.bg

Abstract. In this article, we propose a solution for refueling vehicles with fuel and electricity, serving as the foundation for constructing a system that ensures efficient vehicle management amidst the structural changes triggered by the "Green Deal". The "Smart Sector Integration" plan, as part of the "Green Deal", envisages the unification of sectors—electricity, fuel, and heating—into a single system. This article introduces a servicing system structure for conventional, hybrid, and electric vehicles. Considering the limitations of the current infrastructure in supporting such systems, we suggest the use of renewable energy sources and the adoption of energy storage systems based on hydrogen fuel cells. These modifications find their technical application in the system proposed by the authors. The "Green Deal", also known as the "Green Pact", represents a set of policy measures proposed by the European Commission aimed at making Europe climate-neutral by 2050. Given this backdrop, the proposal is timely and pertinent, looking forward to future infrastructure changes to meet the requirements of the European Union. An investigation into the current state of the electric vehicle fleet in Bulgaria, its expansion, and future development was conducted based on research findings in more developed European countries. We studied the performance of various types of photovoltaic systems, constructed using two different technologies in different geographical regions of Bulgaria. Additionally, the potential for energy storage from fog-electric power stations using hydrogen fuel cells was explored. Analytical, experimental, and digital modeling methods were employed for the research. The studies and results indicate that, to meet the resources for the growing fleet of electric vehicles under a lagging energy infrastructure, such systems need to be developed. The team has specifically focused on this direction, presenting their conclusions and recommendations in the context of the transport sector's development in the Republic of Bulgaria. This system should be established near one of the busiest highways in Bulgaria.

Keywords: Electric vehicles · Charging stations · Renewable energy sources

1 Introduction

Transportation is key to the economy, ensuring efficient consumption, supply of raw materials, and production. Air pollution, mainly from vehicles with internal combustion engines, poses severe risks, emitting pollutants like nitrogen oxides and hydrocarbons. This pollution leads to various diseases affecting vital organs. Rising fuel prices also stress our diminishing oil reserves.

© The Author(s), under exclusive license to Springer Nature Switzerland AG 2023
B. Shishkov and A. Lazarov (Eds.): ICTRS 2023, CCIS 1990, pp. 90–103, 2023.
https://doi.org/10.1007/978-3-031-49263-1_7

The environmental concerns and energy crisis have driven car manufacturers towards hybrid and electric vehicles. Currently, wind and solar energy fulfill only a small portion of our energy needs. Despite advancements, replacing fossil fuels with carbon-neutral sources in the next few decades seems unlikely. Addressing challenges like energy storage during low sunlight or wind periods is crucial, and developing efficient batteries remains problematic [15, 18–20].

Future transportation will feature a mix of electric, hybrid, fuel cell, and traditional vehicles, adjusted to specific needs. Despite the rise of electric vehicles, the internal combustion engine remains vital in many configurations. However, the fast growth of electric vehicles challenges energy networks in developed countries, causing overloads and quality degradation [2, 21–23].

In line with environmental concerns over global warming and emissions, shipping industries are focusing on limiting NOx, SOx, and CO2 emissions. Electric ship engines can reduce ocean pollution and combat high oil prices. The EC mandates a 40% emission reduction by 2030 for shipping companies, highlighting the expected surge in electric and hybrid maritime vehicles between 2019–2029.

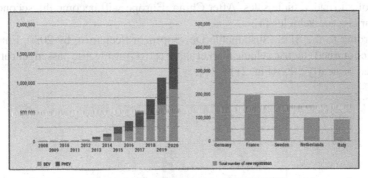

Fig. 1. Availability of electrified vehicles in Europe from 2008–2020 and the top 5 countries for standard new registrations in 2020. Source: [4].

The European Green Deal aims to achieve climate neutrality by 2050. To accelerate the adoption of electric vehicles, European CO2 standards for 2020/21 require car manufacturers to attain a certain percentage of electric vehicle sales, emphasizing the push for greener transport solutions in Europe.

The number of electric vehicles (EVs) has surged dramatically over recent years, reaching 1 million units in 2020, according to the European Alternative Fuels Observatory (EAFO) [4]. Including PHEVs (Plugin Hybrid Electric Vehicles), the count of "electrified vehicles" surpasses 1.5 million, to which more than 100,000 utility vehicles and 4,500 buses should be added. Over 8% of new registrations are related to electric vehicles.

Germany leads in electric vehicle sales, followed by France and Sweden. When considering the percentage of EV sales, Central European countries still exhibit slow growth rates, whereas Northern European nations are at the forefront, with Norway leading by over 30% [13].

This data offers a clear picture of the rising popularity of electric vehicles over the past decade. A chart (Fig. 1) showcases that global purchases from 2012 and projections up to the end of 2021 indicate a 51-fold increase.

Among the primary types of electric vehicles are:

- PHEV (Plugin Hybrid Electric Vehicle): This is a plug-in hybrid electric car that operates using a combination of an electric motor and a battery pack on one hand, and an internal combustion engine on the other. This setup allows them to function either in tandem or independently.
- BEV- (Battery Electric Vehicles): These are vehicles powered solely by an electric motor and a battery. They do not have an internal combustion engine.

In the Global EV Outlook 2020, the International Energy Agency (IEA) describes two global scenarios for the development of e-mobility by 2030: the "Stated Policies Scenario" (STEPS) and the "Sustainable Development Scenario" (SDS) [4].

According to the STEPS data, the global fleet of electric vehicles will increase from 8 million in 2019 to approximately 140 million vehicles by 2030 [4].

By 2030, electric vehicle sales will reach nearly 25 million vehicles, accounting for 16% of all road vehicle sales. After China, Europe will become the second-largest market for electric vehicles [4].

According to the SDS (Sustainable Development Scenario), by 2030, Europe will achieve a combined electric vehicle market share (covering electric passenger cars, buses, and trucks) of nearly 50% (Fig. 2) [4, 10].

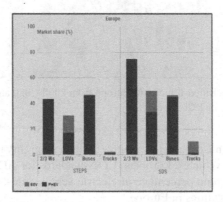

Fig. 2. Share of electric vehicles in car sales in Europe, 2030. Source: [4].

The growth of electric vehicles to 44 million by 2030 demands not just more vehicles but also a robust charging infrastructure. Funding is as crucial as building charging stations. The European Green Deal is shaping EU policy on alternative fuel infrastructure and its financing. These decisions will guide the EU's refueling infrastructure plans.

To support the electric vehicle boom, especially in areas with weaker energy infrastructures, we must build systems beyond urban centers. Charging infrastructure in cities is vital, as home charging is often restricted. Solutions include home or company-based charging, standard public stations, fast-charging stations, or designated EV points.

A smart charging model has been tested, which can minimize grid stress during peak times. Electric vehicles, especially those with larger batteries, are inclined to charge during low-cost electricity periods. This approach could significantly cut energy and infrastructure costs, based on data-driven analysis of charging point locations [24, 25].

Fast and ultra-fast charging is mainly for extended trips, especially on highways, while slow and standard charging is often used for short-term needs or by those without home or workplace charging access. Figures 3 and 4 show that charging points tripled, and charging station capacity quadrupled. In 2020, fast and ultra-fast charging made up around 15% and 5% of all charging points. They represented about 30% of the total power capacity, underlining their amplified importance in the charging infrastructure.

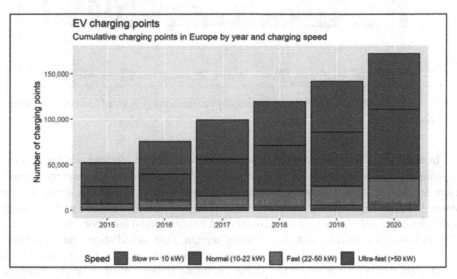

Fig. 3. Data on the number of installed electric vehicle charging points by year and charging speed (data as of November 30, 2020). Source: [1].

Charging infrastructure development is vital for the transition to electric vehicles (EVs) aiming for near-zero emissions by 2050. The EU aims to make EV charging as easy as refueling traditional cars. However, EV adoption depends on charging infrastructure, and infrastructure investments need clarity on EV growth. Charging stations must cater to current and future EV demands, convert grid electricity for EVs, track usage, and provide security and information.

Given urban constraints, charging stations can be:

Level 1: for home use.

Level 2: public stations at parking lots, transport hubs, and corporate areas.

Level 3: fast charging, 10–30 min, with buffer batteries and bidirectional energy flow.

To provide supplementary power and reduce its intake from the main power grid, these charging stations should also integrate renewable energy sources into their system.

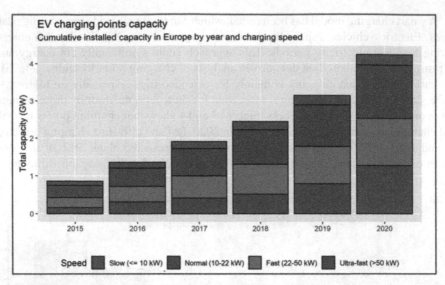

Fig. 4. Data on installed electric vehicle capacity by year and charging speed (data as of November 30, 2020). Source: [1].

In addition to the aforementioned method of restoring an electric vehicle's energy capacity by connecting it to an external power source, there also exists a battery replacement technology. The swapping process is automated and carried out at specialized stations within a timeframe of 3 to 10 min. The implementation of this technology necessitates the adherence to certain constraints: batteries must have consistent mechanical and electrical characteristics, including weight, size, installation and connection method, voltage, and connectivity. If any discrepancies exist, an adequate number of installation stations must be set up. These swapping stations need to be pre-equipped with the requisite batteries and also have provisions for recharging the removed batteries. While this technology offers immense convenience for electric vehicle owners, it comes at a premium cost.

One of the most significant barriers to the widespread adoption of electric vehicles is the lack of charging stations, which would reassure drivers that they can "refuel" anywhere rather than being stranded midway. Global manufacturers are seeking ways to construct a new and expand the existing charging network while simultaneously increasing production.

A prime example of this initiative can be seen in the infrastructure established by Tesla (Fig. 5).

Tesla owners benefit from an exclusive "Supercharger" network. The developmental map of Tesla's charging stations indicates that by 2016, the Balkans will feature approximately 20 supercharger sites. This burgeoning charging infrastructure will enable a seamless journey in a Tesla electric vehicle from Central Europe to Istanbul, further extending into the Asian part of Turkey [5].

Tesla vehicles are distinguished by their extended range. For instance, the Model S can traverse up to 420 km without needing a recharge. Given that these superchargers

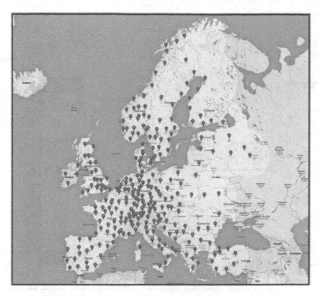

Fig. 5. Map of Tesla charging stations. Source: [5].

can refuel a vehicle in just about 30 min, it signifies a genuinely rapid and hassle-free journey for those in possession of such vehicles [6], echoing the importance of efficient charging solutions as previously discussed.

2 Materials and Methods

For the conducted research, analytical, experimental, and digital simulation methods were employed.

The system proposed by the authors offers the flexibility of payment either before or after the delivery. These are the so-called daytime and nighttime modes of operation. During the day, drivers pull up to the refueling station, refuel their vehicles, and then make payment at the counter inside the building. At night, in the absence of staff, customers first register their payment at the self-service terminal before proceeding to refuel their vehicles.

The pumps and storage tanks are managed by a forecourt controller, which in turn is governed by a computer system. The aim is to ensure that all transactions are recorded and paid for. A new transaction cannot commence at a particular pump if the preceding one hasn't been settled [11, 12].

Connecting to the previously discussed topic, this illustrates the significance of integrating efficient payment systems with the evolving infrastructure of charging stations for electric vehicles.

This concept, albeit relatively old, has been augmented with new elements. An electric vehicle charging station can be connected following a specific protocol similar to a fuel station and can be governed by a forecourt controller.

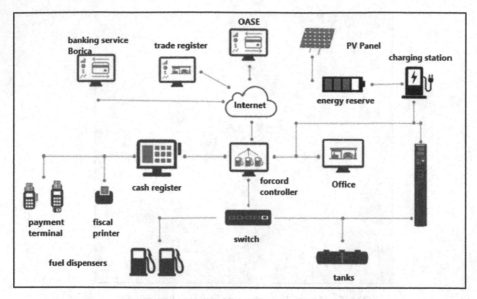

Fig. 6. Structure of the vehicle charging fiscal system. [Compiled by the authors].

In this scenario, electricity bills can be settled through all possible payment methods recognized by the fiscal system, including via self-service devices.

Charging devices equipped with an integrated card reader and the ability to wirelessly connect to the internet are also gaining significant traction. They simplify the configuration to the utmost. However, the need for a robust power source remains crucial.

As depicted in the diagram (Fig. 6), the charging station draws energy from photovoltaic panels. Modern photovoltaic cells do not have the requisite power generation to facilitate charging directly. This is why a large-capacity battery is integrated into the system, where all the electricity produced by the photovoltaic system is stored.

Linking this to the earlier discussion, it emphasizes the importance of integrating renewable energy sources and efficient payment systems in the development and optimization of electric vehicle charging infrastructure.

Repurposing old automotive batteries is a viable approach. While they typically lose their ability to deliver high impulse currents after approximately 3 years of use, they experience only minimal capacity loss. Hence, they can be effectively utilized as energy storage units. In the context of the evolving electric vehicle ecosystem, this strategy not only promotes sustainability by giving batteries a second life but also potentially offers a cost-effective solution for energy storage in various applications, including support for electric vehicle charging stations, particularly those powered by intermittent renewable energy sources like solar panels [7, 16, 17].

The core components of the system include:

- Point of Sale Terminal (POS): A computer operating under the specialized software, NSYS OilSys;
- Office Computer: Equipped with specialized software, NSYS Warehouse;

- Forecourt Controller: A computer and specialized hardware, NSYS CRK2–12, used to manage fuel dispensers and storage tanks;
- Network Switch: Standard equipment ensuring network connectivity for all devices on the premises;
- Fuel Dispensers and Storage Tanks: Vital components for the storage and delivery of fuel;
- Fiscal Printer: A mandatory device for recording sales in compliance with Bulgarian legislation;
- Payment Terminals: Devices dedicated to processing card payments;
- This integrated system ensures seamless operations and interactions between its components, providing efficiency, security, and compliance with regulatory requirements in the fuel dispensing industry.

3 Results

In the article, the team proposes an electric vehicle charging system at charging stations based on the following algorithm:

1. Internet Connectivity: The facility is connected to external operators and institutions via the internet. Through the trade register, there's a direct link to the Bulgarian state body, ensuring that company data is verified when issuing invoices.
2. Borika: This banking institution verifies both debit and credit card transactions during payments.
3. OASF: A Belgian card operator, it facilitates the validation of international fuel cards.
4. Remote Self-Service Device: This system comes equipped with its own fiscal printer, card terminal, and bill acceptor. It allows for unstaffed operation, enabling users to self-serve.
5. Photovoltaic Panels: These panels generate electricity from the sun. The energy storage is handled by a high-capacity battery, preserving the collected energy.
6. Charging Station: This is the device that charges the vehicle.

Photovoltaic electric vehicle charging stations produce sufficient energy to charge two electric vehicles. The energy is harvested from daylight using photovoltaic modules (PV - Photovoltaic System) and is stored in a rechargeable battery. This sustainable approach leverages renewable energy sources, making the electric vehicle charging process even more environmentally friendly.

The components of the charging station include:

- Photovoltaic Panels: These are attached to a lightweight aluminum structure using appropriate bolt connections for supporting beams. Each panel features a terminal box with instructions on output polarity and connects to a terminal using specialized DC connectors. If snow coverage exceeds 10 cm, it is advisable to clear the photovoltaic roof so that the system can continue to operate normally and harness the necessary electricity from the sun.
- DC Terminal: This serves as a connection between the photovoltaic panels and the charge controller. It incorporates 16 A capacity fuses to protect the photovoltaic panels and to interrupt the power supply to the charge controller when necessary.

- Charge Controller: This component automatically adjusts the battery charge level received from the photovoltaic panels. It is designed to protect the battery from both overcharging and deep discharging. To ensure this, it features built-in protection against short circuits and reverse current during nighttime.

The integration of these components ensures an efficient and sustainable system for electric vehicle charging, leveraging the power of solar energy while also incorporating safety features. This represents a green solution to the growing demand for EV charging infrastructure, promising to both protect the environment and ensure reliable operation.
Let's break down these components:

- Sinusoidal Inverter: This device converts the stored electrical energy from the battery cells into a form suitable for charging electric vehicles. It has a feature to connect to the electrical grid and, if necessary, an external generator. It also comes equipped with an output for remote control and monitoring. Such inverters are crucial in transforming the DC energy stored in batteries to the AC energy most electric vehicles require for charging.
- Rechargeable Battery: This is where the energy harnessed by the photovoltaic modules is stored. Its casing is airtight, making it maintenance-free. It's protected against both deep discharge and overcharging. It's housed inside a metal cabinet, shielding it from direct environmental exposures. The battery's capacity is designed to charge two electric vehicles, ensuring that even on days with minimal sunlight, there is enough stored energy for vehicle charging.
- Charging Pillar (or Charging Station): This is used for the controlled charging of electric vehicles, with integrated rectifiers to regulate the charge. It provides a current of 220V, a frequency of 50Hz, and a power of 16A. It's operated via a contactless access card, providing users with a secure and convenient method to initiate charging. There are provisions for account top-up via a coin-operated system, payment card, or by paying for the service via SMS. This ensures that multiple payment methods can be facilitated, catering to various user preferences. The charging pillar also comes equipped with protection against power failure in the absence of a consumer and after full charging. An automated system manages the turning on and off of lights during the night. Moreover, once charging is complete, a message can be sent to the user, informing them of the same.

This setup not only ensures efficient charging of electric vehicles but also incorporates various user-centric features, making the charging process convenient and seamless. With multiple payment options and automated features like lighting control and messaging, the user experience is significantly enhanced.

In the operation of the charging system for electric vehicles, several challenges have been identified:

- The plethora of payment options, predominantly utilizing diverse Radio-Frequency IDentification cards (RFID).
- A lack of preliminary data concerning the status of the charging stations.
- Confusion amongst users due to a diversity of choices combined with inadequate information provision.

To address these challenges, the following best practices are recommended:

- Standardization of the charging systems and the supporting infrastructure.
- Implementing payment options such as credit cards, SMS, or other widely-accepted methods.
- Providing real-time updates on the status of charging stations via a centralized online platform.
- Enhancing communication between different systems.
- Simplifying on-board functions for charging electric vehicles. The recording was made on 21.09. at 1:20 p.m. The upper three graphs show the mains voltages, and the lower three the currents of an inverter with number 4 from transformer 1. It works with a current of about 40A. After the occurrence of the event, it is seen how the inverter currents increase and how they recover after the voltage is restored.

The photovoltaic charging station operates autonomously and functions in an automated mode. To charge electric vehicles, it is necessary to connect the vehicle's contact with the station's contact using an extension cord equipped with the appropriate connectors, cross-section, and insulation. Available connecting contacts are indicated alternately on the charging column's display [8].

The charging process is facilitated using a contactless card. When charging is activated, a "CHARGING" message is displayed alongside the selected charging port. Periodically, the display shows the amount of energy expended for a specific charge session. The power supply is automatically interrupted when there is a disconnection between the electric vehicle and the charging column, or when the vehicle's battery is fully (100%) charged. Should an electrical shock occur, the charging process halts automatically. If communication is lost, reinitiating the charging process is again executed via the contactless card.

Over the course of a year, the station facilitates the charging of 1,440 electric vehicles and 3,800 electric scooters with green energy. Given a travel distance of 50 km on a single charge, the annual reduction in harmful emissions is estimated to be approximately 10.5 tons/year. In addition to this primary environmental benefit, a secondary effect is realized in the form of reduced harmful emissions stemming from the generation of electric power through solar radiation, amounting to 3,800 kWh/year.

4   Discussion

The proliferation of charging stations is intrinsically linked to the presence of electric vehicles (EVs). Currently, the number of EVs in operation is too limited to craft a comprehensive charging program. Another challenge faced is the lack of a unified standardization system for certain components of charging stations and electric vehicle connectors. It is anticipated that in the future, the large-scale construction of charging stations and servicing of vehicles from various brands will be standardized.

Global trends unequivocally suggest that the development of zero-emission electric vehicles is the inevitable direction towards addressing environmental challenges [9]. However, the widespread adoption of electric vehicles in urban environments is largely contingent on the necessary infrastructure for their electric recharging.

A practical and efficient solution to this challenge is the solar-powered charging eco-stations for electric vehicles (see Fig. 7, 8, 9) [3]. These are autonomous entities that draw power not from the grid but from their integrated photovoltaic systems. They do not necessitate any auxiliary infrastructure like substations, cable power supply, electrical panels, etc. Furthermore, they can operate independently anywhere, be it in urban settings or on highways.

Fig. 7. 5 kW Eco-Charging Station built in Sofia, Darvenitsa district in 2011. Source: [14].

Fig. 8. Charging pillar with integrated rectifiers for charging control. Provides current with a voltage of 220V, frequency of 50Hz, and power of 16A. Managed using a contactless access card. Source: [14].

In addition, photovoltaic charging stations for electric vehicles facilitate the direct use of electricity generated from solar radiation, circumventing energy losses associated with transmission through the distribution grid. This completes the cycle of charging electric vehicles, reinforcing them as an environmentally friendly and cost-effective mode of public transportation.

To effectively cater to the rising demand for electricity without overburdening the existing infrastructure, it's imperative to integrate hydrogen fuel cells into the system. These cells can convert the excess energy from photovoltaic panels during periods of underutilization in daylight hours. During nighttime hours, when there's an increased need for charging a larger number of electric vehicles and electricity demand surges, the stored hydrogen can be reconverted by the fuel cells into additional electricity to bolster the system's capacity.

Fig. 9. Battery pack installed in a metal cabinet with a battery capacity for charging two vehicles. Source: [14].

5 Conclusions

An analysis of the charging infrastructure in Europe, globally, and especially in Bulgaria has highlighted various challenges. Many of these can be circumvented by employing advanced digital technologies in the field of hydrogen energy, as posited by the authors of the proposed system. The introduction of such systems, put forth by the team, aligns significantly with the objectives set in the "Green Deal" and fosters the progression of the "Circular Economy". As Bulgaria is in the nascent stages of developing its charging infrastructure, it is imperative to sidestep issues that have arisen in other EU nations.

This paper introduces an innovative solution for an intelligent vehicle charging system. This system not only incorporates contemporary digital technologies but also mainstream technologies that harness renewable energy sources. By merging these two cutting-edge technologies, the authors aspire to make a modest stride, using digital transformation, towards embracing the principles of the circular economy as mandated by the contemporary "Green Directive".

References

1. Falchetta, G., Noussan M.: Electric vehicle charging network in Europe: an accessibility and deployment trends analysis. Transp. Res. Part D: Transp. Environ. **94**, 102813 (2021)
2. Surkov, M.A., Obukhov, S.G., Plotnikov, I.A., Sumarokova, L.P., Popov, M.M., Baidali, S.A.: Evaluation of the feasibility of using photovoltaic installations for power supply to remote consumers in the climatic conditions of the Russian North Federations. Internet J. "SCIENCE" **8**(4) (2016)
3. Seymenliyski, K.D., Dolchinkov, R.S., Simionov, R.R.: Application of European Union directives on energy efficiency of building systems in practical training of students in RES technologies. In: ICTRS '21, p. 43–47, November 15, 16 (2021). ACM ISBN 978–1–4503–9018–7/21
4. European Alternative Fuels Observatory. https:eafo.eu. Accessed 12 Dec 2021
5. https:eafo.eu. Accessed 12 Dec. 2021
6. Seymenliyski K.: Operational Management - New Challenges, pp. 183–191, BSU Yearbook (2020). volume XLII, ISSN: 1311–221X
7. Bobyl, A.V., et al.: Renormalized model for solar power plants economic efficiency evaluation, Izvestiya Akademii Nauk, Energy, No. 6 (2017)

8. Gabderakhmanova, T.S.: LB Director, analysis of autonomous power supply schemes based on renewable sources of energy. Promyshlennaya energetika (4), 48–51 (2015)
9. Varbov, T.K.: Some specific problems with photovoltaic systems connected to the electricity distribution network, Author's abstract of a dissertation for awarding the educational and scientific degree "DOCTOR", Gabrovo (2015)
10. Energy Development Forecast for Peace and Russia 2019/edited. In: Makarova, A.A., Mitrovoi, T.A., Kulagina, V.A., INEI RAN–Moscow School of Management Skolkovo – Moscow, p. 210 (2019). ISBN 978–5–91438–028–8
11. Ratner, S.V., Aksyuk, T.D. Foreign experience of stimulating microgenerations based on renewable energy sources: organizational and economic aspects, Scientific and technical reports of SPbGPU. Econ. Sci. **10**(4) (2017)
12. Obretenov, D., Simeon Iliev, S.: Prospects for the development of internal combustion engines. In: Proceedings of University of Ruse - 2021, vol. 60, book 4.3 FRI-2.209–1-TMS-05 :25–29 (2021)
13. Transport & Environment Published: January 2020 © 2020 European Federation for Transport and Environment AISBL (2020)
14. http://energy-review.bg
15. Rodrigue, J.-P., Comtois, C., Slack, B.: The Geography of Transport Systems (2016). https://doi.org/10.4324/9781315618159
16. Simionov, R., Mollova, S., Dolchinkov, R., Integrated laboratory complex. In: 2020 43rd International Convention on Information, Communication and Electronic Technology, MIPRO 2020 - Proceedingsthis link is disabled, 2020, ISSN 1847–3946, pp. 1567–1572, 9245339 (2020)
17. Matsankov M., Ivanova, M.: Selection of optimal variant of hybrid system under conditions of uncertainty. In: The 2nd International Conference on Electrical Engineering and Green EnergyRoma, Italy, June 28–30 (2019). https://www.e3s-conferences.org/articles/e3sconf/abs/2019/41/contents/contents.html, E3S Web of Conferences, 2019, 115, 01007
18. Seymenliyski, K., Letskovska, S., Simionov, R., Zaerov, E.: Electrical equipment impact on the environment and quantity factor measurement. In: ICTRS '18, ACM International Conference Proceeding Series, Proceedings of the Seventh International Conference on Telecommunications and Remote Sensing, pp. 41–44, October 8–9 (2018). Barcelona, Spain. ISBN: 978–1–4503–6580–2, https://doi.org/10.1145/3278161.3278168
19. Letskovska, S., Zaerov, E., Seymenliyski, K., Mikhov, S.: Environmental influence on renewable sources productivity. In: International Conference on High Technology for Sustainable Development (HiTech 2018), Proceedings, 2018, 8566343 Sofia, Bulgaria 11–14 June 2018, pp.209–212 (2018). IEEE Catalog Number: ISBN: 978–1–5386–7040–8
20. Seymenliyski, K., Zaerov, E., Simionov, R., Letskovska, S.: Reducing the environmental impact of electrical installations. In: International Conference on High Technology for Sustainable Development (HiTech 2018) Sofia, Bulgaria 11–14 June 2018, Proceedings, 2018, 8566396, pp.206–209 (2018). IEEE Catalog Number: ISBN: 978–1–5386–7040–8
21. Mollova, S., Seymenliyski, K., Letskovska, S., Simionov, R., Zaerov, E.: Training system for the study of computer clusters. In: International Conference on High Technology for Sustainable Development (HiTech 2019) Sofia, Bulgaria, ISBN (Print-On-Demand): 978–1–7281–4557–0, ISBN (Online): 978–1–7281–4556–3, IEEE Catalog Number: CFP19Q62-POD, Proceedings of Papers 9128124, pp. 134–137 (2019)
22. Seymenliyski, K., Letskovska, S., Zaerov, E., Simionov, R., Mollova, S.: Laboratory system for monitoring and forecasting the parameters of sea waves. In: International Conference on High Technology for Sustainable Development (HiTech 2019) Sofia, Bulgaria, ISBN: 978–1–7281–4557–0, ISBN (Online): 978–1–7281–4556–3, IEEE Catalog Number: CFP19Q62-POD, Proceedings of Papers, 9128243, pp. 138–142 (2019)

23. Zaerov, E., Letskovska, S., Seymenliyski, K., Simionov, R.: PV system monitoring by IoT in smart university. In: ICTRS '20, October 5–6, 2020, Milan, Italy, SCOPUS ISBN: 978–1–4503–7730–0, pp. 44–49 (2020)

24. Seymenliyski, K., Letskovska, S., Zaerov, E., Simionov, R., Mollova, S.: Laboratory complex for training and research of PV-technologies. In: International Conference on Technics, Technologies and Education, ICTTE 2020, ISSN 1314–9474, November 4–6 2020, Faculty of Technics and Technologies of Yambol, Trakia University of Stara Zagora, Bulgaria IOP Conf. Ser.: Mater. Sci. Eng. 1031, 012121 (2021). https://iopscience.iop.org/article/10.1088/1757-899X/1031/1/012121

25. Letskovska, S., Seymenliyski, K.: Renewable energy sources and pricing of electrical power. Journal of Energy and Power Engineering is published monthly in hard copy (ISSN1934–8975) and online (ISSN 1934–7367) by David Publishing Company, US, 2014; Volume 8, Number 5, May 2014(Serial Number 78), p. 896–902, Database of EBSCO Massachusetts USA; Google Scholar; CiteFactor (USA); Electronic Journals Library; Database of Cambridge Science Abstracts (CSA), USA

26. Matsankov M.: Study of the short-circuit currents in branches of distribution networks with trilateral power suplliy. In: TechSys 2019" – Engineering, Technologies and Systems – Technical University of Sofia, Plovdiv branch 16–18 May 2019, IOP Conference Series: Materials Science and Engineering, **618**(1), 012020 (2019). https://iopscience.iop.org/issue/1757-899X/618/1

Short Papers

Short Papers

Acoustic System for the Detection and Recognition of Drones

Ivan Garvanov[1], Penka Pergelova[1(✉)], and Nurym Nurdaulet[2]

[1] University of Library Studies and Information Technologies, Sofia, Bulgaria
{i.garvanov,p.pergelova}@unibit.bg
[2] Al-Farabi Kazakh National University, Almaty, Kazakhstan

Abstract. The paper proposes and studies a UAV detection algorithm based on acoustic signature recognition. The recognition of the acoustic signals of the UAV is carried out in the spectral domain of the signal after the evaluation of the frequency characteristics of the audio signal. The proposed algorithm can be used for real-time UAV detection.

Keywords: UAV detection · acoustic processing · spectrogram

1 Introduction

Unmanned aerial vehicles (UAVs), also called drones, are increasingly used in everyday life. They are used in areas such as logistics and transportation, surveillance of areas and objects with the possibility of photo and video recording, agriculture, police, military missions, and many others. Drones are useful because they can reach remote locations and spend a long time in the sky. Due to the low price, high productivity and utility, easy maintenance and management, drones are finding more and more applications. However, the increase in their use both for military and civilian purposes brings with it a threat to airspace security that can put people, property, key areas, and buildings at risk. These threats can be caused by both incompetent UAV management and deliberate attacks that can cause significant damage [1, 2]. In recent years, we have witnessed quite a few UAV accidents, some of which are unintentional and some of which are intentional [3]. There has been an increase in cases of drones flying close to airports, causing temporary closures of airports [4]. Drones can be used for terrorist attacks, crashes, delivery of drugs, weapons, and other illegal goods [3].

To protect the population from misuse and unauthorized use of drones, it is necessary to regulate rules for their use. The rapid development of the drone industry requires that the regulatory framework for the use of drones be updated in a timely manner. These measures will reduce unskilled drone piloting and unwanted accidents, but they cannot prevent deliberate criminal or terrorist attacks. To combat the illegal actions of drones, it is necessary to develop anti-drone systems to counter and minimize unwanted incidents. For this purpose, it is necessary to design and develop effective systems that detect the presence of drones in space, classify them, track them, recognize them and, if necessary,

© The Author(s), under exclusive license to Springer Nature Switzerland AG 2023
B. Shishkov and A. Lazarov (Eds.): ICTRS 2023, CCIS 1990, pp. 107–116, 2023.
https://doi.org/10.1007/978-3-031-49263-1_8

counter them. The task of discovering these objects is of paramount importance for subsequent actions. Therefore, it is essential to establish an effective UAV detection system. In practice, several types of technical solutions to this issue are used and applied, namely: drone detection using radar, radio frequency (RF) signal detection, visual and acoustic detection [5–9].

Radar sensors are expensive and are used to detect relatively large UAVs implemented with radio-opaque materials flying at high speed on high-altitude ballistic trajectories. Radar sensors work well regardless of environmental factors and illumination levels, but they do not have good classification capabilities [5]. Radar detection principles can be used for all possible configurations such as monostatic, bistatic and forward scattering radars. An RF approach to drone detection and classification is applicable to radio-controlled drones or drones maintaining radio communication with the control center. Using the radio frequency characteristics of drones, they can be detected, identified, and categorized.

Using Software Defined Radio (SDR) to process drone radio signals is a cheap and convenient way to detect and identify drones. By receiving the signals from the drone's radio controller by means of receiving antennas with high signal gain in combination with highly sensitive receiving systems, the detection of drones at long distances is achieved. In the presence of appropriate equipment to detect the radio control signals of the drone, it is possible to jam them, blocking the control of the drone, or to emit more powerful radio control signals, thereby taking over the control of the drone by the anti-drone system.

Drone detection can also be accomplished using video surveillance cameras, allowing medium detection range and acceptable localization accuracy. This method is cheap and easy to implement but is not effective during the dark part of the day or when visibility is reduced due to clouds or pollution. This shortcoming can be compensated using thermal cameras, which are not affected by illumination, but are dependent on infrared radiation from heated bodies [10].

Acoustic sensors are another possible method of drone detection and can be implemented with low-cost microphones that listen to the airwaves and pick up the distinctive sound characteristics of the drones' various rotors. These systems are effective both during the day and in poor visibility conditions, but a significant drawback for them is the relatively short detection distance of the drone. Acoustic systems have good applicability for small monitoring areas such as inter-block spaces in urban environments. The increase in the working area of the acoustic system is achieved using many sensors scattered over a large area [11, 12].

With the development of intelligent systems and artificial intelligence, and in particular machine learning and deep learning methods, new technical solutions for drone detection and recognition have been proposed in recent years. These technologies increase the probability of correct UAV detection and increase the performance of anti-drone systems by achieving good results in object recognition accuracy.

This paper proposes and studies a method for drone detection and recognition by processing acoustic signals and evaluating its frequency characteristics. It is structured as follows: Sect. 2 examines the acoustic characteristics generated by drones, Sect. 3 analyzes the Fourier transform as the main method for obtaining the spectrum of the audio signal, Sect. 4 presents some of the audio features needed for drone classification, Sect. 5 reviews the obtained results from acoustic signal processing and draws conclusions and recommendations for future research.

2   Acoustic Signals Generated by UAV

Reliable detection and classification of UAVs is essential for the effective operation of anti-drone systems. The sounds generated by drones in flight are derived from both their engines and the type of cargo carried on board of UAV. With appropriate sound processing, it is possible to distinguish specific sound characteristics and to recognize both the type of UAV and the type of payload it carries [13]. Using a sound antenna array or a dispersed multi-sensor acoustic system with specific signal processing, it is possible to estimate the location of the drone very accurately in space as well as determine the distance to it. The detection and recognition of UAV using acoustic signals allows timely activation of the security system. For a more effective UAV countermeasure, it is required to recognize the type or model of the drone as well as the type of its payload with high reliability. Accurate determination of the drone's coordinates is essential for countering the drone [14].

In our opinion, using the acoustic sensor method for drone detection and recognition is the most suitable to solve these problems from a technical point of view. Examining the sound signatures of different types of drones would allow finding specific assessments and technical capabilities to determine the type of drone as well as its payload. This is possible because different models of drones have different geometric shapes and use different motors that generate different sounds with specific frequency characteristics. Also, if drones of the same model carry loads of different shapes and weights, they will make different sounds. Considering all the advantages and disadvantages of acoustic sensor systems, we conclude that they are very suitable for use in the inter-block space in urban conditions [15]. The accumulation of a big database of acoustic signals from different types of drones carrying different loads will allow fine-tuning of the algorithms we develop and will lead to the most effective solution to the given task.

3   Spectral Characteristics of the Signal

All sound signals in nature are characterized by specific frequency and amplitude characteristics, which are used in practice to analyze and recognize sounds. To evaluate these characteristics, audio signals can be represented as a set of sinusoidal signals with different frequencies and amplitudes. The mathematical method of decomposing a signal into its individual components is known as the Fourier transform. The generated sinusoids from the Fourier transform in time signal processing are a complex quantity whose imaginary part represents the phase shift of the pure sinusoid and whose absolute value is the value of the corresponding frequency component.

Working with discrete signal values requires the application of the Discrete Fourier Transform (DFT). The most efficient method for calculating the DFT that allows signal transformation from the time domain to the frequency domain is the Fast Fourier Transform (FFT). It is used to represent the signal in the frequency domain and is implemented with the following equation [16]:

$$X(j\omega) = \int_{-\infty}^{\infty} x(t)e^{-j\omega t}dt \tag{1}$$

The mathematical representation of the DFT, which is used to transform the signal from the time domain to the frequency domain, is expressed by the following equation:

$$X[k] = \sum_{n=0}^{N-1} x[n]e^{-j\frac{2\pi}{N}kn} \tag{2}$$

The discrete signal transformation can be represented by complex numbers and complex trigonometric functions. If we apply FFT to an audio file of a certain length, we will only get information about the frequency and amplitude of that audio signal. Processing an audio signal by frequency and amplitude alone is not enough to create a data stream for machine learning and subsequent sound recognition. For this purpose, audio signal processing requires the acquisition of a spectrogram of the audio signal and the parallel accumulation of information about its time domain and frequency domain parameters. The spectrogram allows the acquisition and analysis of extended information about this audio signal. It is used to represent the frequency spectrum of a signal as a function of time.

The spectrogram is obtained using the Short-time Fourier transform (STFT) and is used to analyze the frequency content of a non-stationary signal changing over time. As is known, the audio signal changes over time, but it can be assumed that this change is not large for short time intervals, which will simplify the processing steps. Dividing the input signal into small time intervals allows to extract from them a stream of information related to their frequency. These parts are called a window of analysis and have a duration of 5 ms for a wideband signal and up to 30 ms for a narrowband signal. Windows are used to create short sound fragments that last only a few milliseconds. If the window is much longer, the signal will fluctuate a lot, and if it is much shorter, then there will not be enough samples to obtain a reliable spectral estimate. The STFT of a signal is calculated by dragging the analysis window over the signal and calculating the DFT of each data segment of the window.

There are different window shapes, the most common being trapezoidal, triangular, polynomial, and sinusoidal. DFT often uses windows of Hann, Gaussian, and Hamming. The window jumps over the original signal so that there is an overlap between adjacent segments of the order of 30%. The DFT result of the window segments is added to a matrix that contains the amplitude and phase for each time and frequency point. By analogy with the DFT, the discrete STFT is defined as:

$$X(n, k) = X(n, \omega)|_{\omega=\frac{2\pi}{N}k} \tag{3}$$

A spectrogram is a graphical representation of the discrete STFT value, usually on a logarithmic scale.

$$S(n, k) = log|X(n, k)|^2 \tag{4}$$

Due to the long duration of the sound signal generated by a drone, as well as the different frequency characteristics of the signal over time, it is preferable to analyze the spectral diagram of the signal being studied.

4 Audio Features

For the correct recognition and identification of audio images, it is necessary to use audio features, which should be efficient, robust, and physically interpretable to obtain a machine processable data representation containing the key properties of the audio signal [16].

While recording an audio signal from a drone, signals coming from the environment and generated by various sources are also recorded, such as: wind, noise from the leaves of trees, passing vehicles, human speech and sounds made by animals and others. Also, the audio signal from the drone is non-stationary in time, it can only be assumed to be stationary for short periods of time on the order of 10–30 ms. This means that the spectrum of the audio signal can be considered practically homogeneous for a few milliseconds.

Processing the audio segments at small time intervals of the order of 20 ms allows obtaining time and frequency characteristics that carry information useful for drone identification. Denoting by $x(n)$ the discrete time representation of a normalized audio recording of a signal, the audio data of each subframe $s(n)$ is given by Eq. (5):

$$s(n) = x(n)w(m - n)$$
$$w(n) = 0.54 - cos\left(\frac{2\pi (m - n)}{L - 1}\right) n \in [0, L) \tag{5}$$

where $w(n)$ is a Hamming window of length L and m its time shift. To compute the raw features and locally characterize the corresponding audio waveform and spectrum shape, each sub-frame $s(n)$ is processed by a bank of specific filters based on the feature algorithms.

A. Time-Domain Signal Features

Time-domain features are used for audio segment extraction. These functions are useful in cases of implementing simple and efficient sound classification algorithms. The most used features are: the Short-Time Energy and the Zero Crossing Rate [16].

- Short Time Energy (STE)

Short-term energy is the most natural feature that has been used in practice. It is a measure of how much signal there is at any one time. Energy is used to discover audio signals, which have higher energy. The energy of a signal is calculated on a short time basis, by window processing, squaring the samples and taking the average [16]. The square root of this result is the engineering quantity, known as the root-mean square (RMS) value. The short-time energy function of an audio frame with length L is defined as:

$$STE = \frac{1}{L} \sum_{n=1}^{L-1} |s(n)|^2 \tag{6}$$

- Zero crossing rate (ZCR)

It is one of feature extraction methods in audio processing to calculate how many times the audio waveform crosses the zero axis. This feature is useful to identify voiced subframe. ZCR is used to discern unvoiced audio. Usually, unvoiced audio has a low short-term energy but a high zero crossing rate. Combining ZCR and STE to prevent low energy unvoiced audio frames from being classified as silent.

$$ZCR = \frac{1}{2L} \sum_{n=0}^{L} |sign(s(n)) - sign(s(n-1))| \tag{7}$$

B. *Frequency-Domain Signal Features.*
To extract frequency domain features, discrete Fourier transform can be used. The most used features are: the Spectral Centroid (SC), the Spectral Roll-Off (SRO), and the Mel Frequency Cepstrum Coefficients [16].

- Spectral Centroid (SC)

The spectral centroid is a measure used in digital signal processing to characterize a spectrum. This feature is a measure of the spectral position, with high values of sounds. The spectral centroid, SC_i of the i-th frame is defined as the center of "gravity" of its spectrum and it is given by the following equation:

$$SC_i = \frac{\sum_{m=0}^{L-1} f(m) X_i(m)}{\sum_{m=0}^{L-1} X_i(m)}$$

$$X_k = \sum_{n=o}^{L-1} s(n) . e^{-j2\pi kn/L} \tag{8}$$

Here, $f(m)$ represents the center frequency of i-th bin with length L and $X_i(m)$ is the amplitude corresponding to that bin in DFT spectrum.

- Spectral Roll-Off (SRO)

The Spectral Roll-Off is defined as the frequency below which 90% is the distribution magnitude is concentrated.

$$SRO = \arg \min_{f_c \in (1,..,N)} \sum_{i=1}^{f_c} m_i \geq 0.9 \sum_{i=1}^{N} m_i \tag{9}$$

where f_c is the Roll-Off frequency and m_i is the magnitude of the i-th frequency component of the spectrum.

- Mel Frequency Cepstrum Coefficients (MFCC)

Mel frequency cepstral coefficients are the discrete cosine transform of the melscaled log-power spectrum. The main steps to compute these M cepstral coefficients are described below.

The M banks of Mel filters are used to map the power spectrum onto the mel-scale. The frequency responses of these filter banks are triangular and equally spaced along the mel-scale.

$$Mel_f = 2.595 log_{10}\left(1 + \frac{f}{700}\right) \qquad (10)$$

After analyzing the subframes into the environmental audio frame, the relative sequences of low-level features are processed statistically on a mid-term time window. The goal is to obtain new salient mid-term features with low sensitivity to the small variations of underlying audio signal. Then, a set of mid-term robust features are aggregated in a global vector that can completely describe the perceptual physical property of the environmental audio frame.

5 Results

To study the proposed algorithm, a set of measurements aimed at accumulating audio signals obtained from a parabolic microphone with high gain and weak audio signal recording capabilities were conducted (Fig. 1). During the experiments, a DJI PHANTOM 3 ADVANCED drone was used. It flies at different distances from the microphone and in different modes of operation. An example recording of an audio signal containing drone sound is shown in Fig. 2. Changing the flight direction and operating mode changes the amplitude and frequency characteristics of the drone audio signal. During the experiment, there is also a light wind, which generates additional noise in the microphone.

Fig. 1. Topology of the experiment

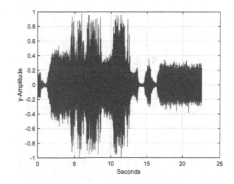

Fig. 2. Audio signal in the time domain

Using a Fourier transform for a short period of time, a spectrum of the sound signal is obtained, which is shown in Fig. 3. This spectrum is a carrier of useful information, but it is a short-term evaluation of the characteristics of the signal, so it is necessary to obtain the spectrum of the signal, which is shown in Fig. 4 and virtualizes the spectral characteristics as a function of time. The spectrum of the signal shows the predominant spectral characteristics of the audio signal, which can be used in subsequent classification of the drone.

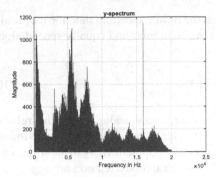

Fig. 3. Spectrum of the audio signal   **Fig. 4.** Spectrogram of the drone's audio signal

Obtaining short-term estimates of audio characteristics and their subsequent averaging is the basis of effective drone recognition and classification. The results Spectral Centroid, Spectral Roll-Off and Mel Frequency Cepstrum Coefficients are shown in Figs. 5, 6, and 7.

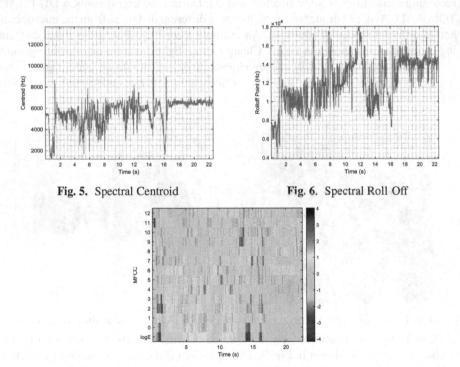

Fig. 5. Spectral Centroid   **Fig. 6.** Spectral Roll Off

Fig. 7. Mel Frequency Cepstrum Coefficients

Given all mid term windows in the environmental audio frame, it is considered a selection of these statistics for the various raw features to generate a vector of mid term features by concatenation. This result is the audio signature vector of the frame which is processed by the classifier for the identification of drone sound.

6 Conclusion and Future Work

This work proposes an algorithm to estimate the parameters of a drone audio signal for the purpose of drone detection and recognition. The proposed algorithm can be improved after applying a self-learning system. In our next developments, an attempt for machine learning and recognition of different drone models in different operating modes will be made.

Acknowledgement. This work was supported by the National Science Program "Security and Defense", which has received funding from the Ministry of Education and Science of the Republic of Bulgaria under the grant agreement № D01-74 /19.05.2022.

References

1. Utebayeva, D., Almagambetov, A., Alduraibi, M., Temirgaliyev, Y., Ilipbayeva, L., Marxuly, S.: Multi-label UAV sound classification using Stacked Bidirectional LSTM. In: Fourth IEEE International Conference on Robotic Computing (IRC), Taichung, Taiwan, pp. 453–458 (2020). https://doi.org/10.1109/IRC.2020.00086
2. Utebayeva, D., Alduraibi, M., Ilipbayeva, L., Temirgaliyev, Y.: Stacked BiLSTM - CNN for multiple label UAV sound classification. In: Fourth IEEE International Conference on Robotic Computing (IRC), Taichung, Taiwan, pp. 470–474 (2020). https://doi.org/10.1109/IRC.2020.00089
3. Drone Crash Database, 4 June 2023. https://dronewars.net/drone-crash
4. McFarland, M.: Airports Scramble to Handle Drone Incidents, 15 June 2019. https://www.cnn.com/2019/03/05/tech/airports-drones/index.html
5. Garvanov, I., Kanev, D., Garvanova, M., Ivanov, V.: Drone detection approach based on radio frequency detector. In: International Conference "Automatics and Informatics" – ICAI 2023, 5–7 October 2023, Varna, Bulgaria (2023)
6. Garvanov, I., Garvanova, M., Ivanov, V., Lazarov, A., Borissova, D., Kostadinov, T.: Detection of unmanned aerial vehicles based on image processing. In: Shishkov, B. (ed.) Proceedings of the Eleventh International Conference on Telecommunications and Remote Sensing – ICTRS 2022, 21–22 November 2022, Sofia, Bulgaria (2022). https://doi.org/10.1007/978-3-031-232 26-8_3
7. Garvanova, M., Ivanov, V.: Quality assessment of defocused image recovery algorithms. In: International Conference on Sensors, Signal and Image Processing – SSIP 2020, 9–11 October 2020, Prague, Czech Republic, pp. 25–30 (2020). https://doi.org/10.1145/3441233.3441242
8. Garvanova, M., Ivanov, V.: Quality assessment of image deburring algorithms. IOP Conf. Ser. Mater. Sci. Eng. **1031**(1), 1–5 (2021). https://doi.org/10.1088/1757-899X/1031/1/012051
9. Behar, V., Kabakchiev, C., Garvanov, I.: Simple algorithms for target detection in FSR using local statistics. In: 14th International Radar Symposium (IRS), Dresden, Germany, pp. 631–636 (2013)
10. Shishkov, B., Garvanova, M.: The societal impacts of drones: a public values perspective. In: Shishkov, B., Lazarov, A. (eds.) International Conference on Telecommunications and Remote Sensing – ICTRS 2022, 21–22 November 2022, Sofia, Bulgaria. CCIS, vol. 1730, pp. 61–71. Springer, Cham (2022). https://doi.org/10.1007/978-3-031-23226-8_5

11. Bernardini, A., Mangiatordi, F., Pallotti E., Capodiferro, L.: Drone detection by acoustic signature identification. In: Proceedings of IS&T International Symposium on Electronic Imaging: Imaging and Multimedia Analytics in a Web and Mobile World, pp. 60–64 (2017). https://doi.org/10.2352/ISSN.2470-1173.2017.10.IMAWM-168

12. Utebayeva, D., Ilipbayeva, L., Matson, E.T.: Practical study of recurrent neural networks for efficient real-time drone sound detection: a review. Drones 7(1), 26 (2023). https://doi.org/10.3390/drones7010026

13. Taha, B., Shoufan, A.: Machine learning-based drone detection and classification: state-of-the-art in research. IEEE Access 7, 138669–138682 (2019). https://doi.org/10.1109/ACCESS.2019.2942944

14. Samaras, S., et al.: Deep learning on multi sensor data for counter UAV applications–a systematic review. Sensors 19(22), 4837 (2019). https://doi.org/10.3390/s19224837

15. Boneva, Y., Ivanov, V.: Improvement of traffic in urban environment through signal timing optimization. In: Dimov, I., Fidanova, S. (eds.) Advances in High Performance Computing. HPC 2019. SCI, vol. 902, pp. 99–107. Springer, Cham (2021). https://doi.org/10.1007/978-3-030-55347-0_9

16. Alexey, P., Olga, P., Natalia, S.: Fast parametric Fourier transform. In: International Conference on Dynamics and Vibroacoustics of Machines (DVM), Samara, Russian Federation, pp. 1–6 (2022). https://doi.org/10.1109/DVM55487.2022.9930933

A Study on Thermal Influence on Adolescents Due to Long-Term Mobile Phone Exposure

Georgi Tsonkov[1], Gabriela Garvanova[2,3], and Daniela Borissova[2,3]([✉])

[1] Elektro Mechanik Sonnenschein GmbH, Schönau am Königssee, Germany
gtsonkov@tsoftcomputers.de
[2] University of Library Studies and Information Technologies, Sofia, Bulgaria
gabigarvanova@abv.bg, dborissova@iit.bas.bg
[3] Institute of Information and Communication Technologies, Bulgarian Academy of Sciences, Sofia, Bulgaria

Abstract. The continuous increase in the use of mobile communication devices, as well as the escalating dependence of people on them, sets the stage for various psychological and physical effects on humans. Conducting comprehensive and in-depth studies on the effects caused by excessive use of mobile devices can be used for the prevention of negative consequences and the improvement of people's quality of life. This paper examines the thermal effects on adolescents caused by prolonged use of mobile phones and, more specifically, by exposure to high-frequency electromagnetic fields.

Keywords: electromagnetic field · Infrared thermography · mobile devices

1 Introduction

The mobile technologies and communications hold a significant place in people's live. The past decades have exerted a powerful influence on their development, leading to a dramatic increase in the number of subscribers and network-connected devices. Along with this trend and all the conveniences and comfort that mobile devices provide, they can also have a substantial negative impact on the mental and physical health of people [1–3]. Over recent years, the data transmission rate has multiplied, making mobile services more attractive and desirable for the people. Conversely, the increasing number of users and connected devices has led to an intense rise in the amount of data transmitted by mobile operators and internet providers. For comparison, in Germany, data transmission from mobile operators has increased by about 40 times between 2010 and 2020 [4]. With the advancement of technology, the frequency band used is continually increasing, with the most used frequencies nowadays ranging from 900 MHz to 5 GHz. The trend is to be increasing up to 300 GHz, which will exceed the lower limit of the internationally defined extremely high radio frequencies [5, 6]. For example, the frequency spectrum of fifth-generation mobile communications (5G) has reached operational frequencies up to 54 GHz, with a tendency for these to increase.

© The Author(s), under exclusive license to Springer Nature Switzerland AG 2023
B. Shishkov and A. Lazarov (Eds.): ICTRS 2023, CCIS 1990, pp. 117–126, 2023.
https://doi.org/10.1007/978-3-031-49263-1_9

As known from physics, signals with higher frequencies attenuate more rapidly during propagation. Consequently, in 5G networks, considering the higher operating frequency, the signal will attenuate more rapidly, necessitating the use of more powerful transmitters with higher amplitude and/or an increased number of base stations. Meanwhile, sources of high-frequency electromagnetic pollution continue to proliferate. The construction of the Starlink satellite system aims to provide global coverage, effectively enabling internet access from any point on Earth [7]. The continuous growth in the number of connected "smart" wireless device leads to an increased load on the radio spectrum with electromagnetic waves (EMWs).

From the preceding discussion, it becomes evident that information technologies, particularly mobile communication technologies, offer convenience and beneficial connectivity and communication possibilities. However, the exponential growth of devices has led to a significant increase in electromagnetic pollution. In this context, the present article will examine and analyze some of the potential effects of generated electromagnetic fields (EMFs) on the human body, with a particular focus on the effects of increased body temperature in the head region during the usage of mobile communication devices.

Section 2 of this study will dedicate special attention to infrared thermography, which forms the foundation of the conducted scientific investigations. Section 3 will describe the results of the conducted experimental studies and analyze the obtained data. In conclusion, recommendations and conclusions will be drawn regarding the usage of mobile communication devices.

2   Infrared Thermography

Infrared thermography registers the energy exchange caused by thermal conductivity, thermal convection, and infrared radiation of a given object. It recreates the instantaneous, static, and steady-state spatial distribution of the heat flow on the observed surface. Everything in nature with a temperature higher than absolute zero emits electromagnetic waves in the infrared range proportional to its temperature. The infrared spectrum used for thermography purposes spans from 14 µm to 780 nm in electromagnetic wave length. Technological advancements in recent decades have made these types of instruments increasingly accessible, popular, and user-friendly. Nowadays, thermal imaging devices find applications in various fields of life, such as medicine, industry, defense, etc. [8, 9].

By measuring the intensity of electromagnetic waves emitted from the surface of an object at a particular moment, its temperature can be determined. This process involves focusing the infrared radiation emitted by the object onto a detector, which converts it into an electrical signal. After processing the signal, a two-dimensional thermal image is obtained. To determine the temperature accurately, several factors must be taken into consideration, as they can significantly influence the measurement accuracy, such as: the material composition of the object's external surface, distance, type of detector used (its specifications), and others.

The energy emitted by an object is proportional to its temperature, as described by Planck's law, which establishes the relationship between temperature and the spectral emission of an ideal black body [8]. This relationship is expressed by the following equation:

$$M_{\lambda s} = \frac{2\pi hc^2}{\lambda^5} \frac{1}{e^{\frac{hc}{\lambda kT}} - 1}$$ (1)

where c is the speed of light, h is Planck's constant, k is Boltzmann's constant, λ represents the wavelength, and T denotes the temperature (°K). The relationship between temperature and wavelength is depicted in Fig. 1 for temperatures of 300 °K, 350 °K, 400 °K, 450 °K, and 500 °K, corresponding to 26.85 °C, 76.85 °C, 126.85 °C, 176.85 °C, and 226.85 °C, respectively. From the figure, it is evident that increasing the wavelength leads to an increase in the intensity of emission, and at the same time, this is associated with the temperature of the body.

A conclusion can be drawn that as the temperature of the ideal black body rises above 550 °C to 580 °C, the wavelength starts to enter the visible range of the electromagnetic spectrum, corresponding to the color red, visible to the human eye. In other words, as the temperature increases, the wavelength decreases [10, 11].

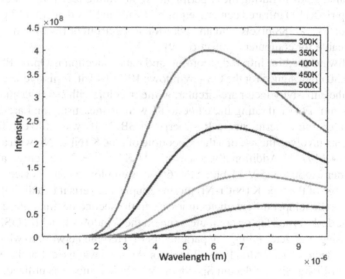

Fig. 1. Emission intensity as a function of wavelength (Color figure online)

3 Experimental Results

The conducted experiments aim to research the impact of electromagnetic waves emitted by mobile devices on children. This is achieved by measuring the temperature changes in the head area during mobile phone usage. The study includes two participants from different age groups (7 years old and 12 years old), and effects are examined for both genders. The selection of participants from different age groups and genders is made to account for possible variations in the results related to the body's water content. The experiments were carried out with strict adherence to specific protocols to avoid any inaccuracies during the tests. A series of measurements were performed, and the article presents the averaged results. Prior consent was obtained from both the children and their parents for conducting the research.

3.1 Rules for Conducting the Experiments

All experiments were conducted in the same room with an ambient temperature of 20–21 °C. Each participant spent 10 min in the room before the start of the experiment for acclimatization, during which they did not carry or use a mobile device or any other device generating EMFs. The duration of the experiment, involving active use of the mobile device, was 20 min. Temperature was recorded immediately before the experiment started and at its conclusion. There was a minimum 45-min interval between two experiments involving the same participant, during which they did not use a mobile phone. The experiments utilized a Huawei P30-G mobile device with a SAR value of 0.7, a signal operational frequency of Downlink 796 MHz, Uplink – 806 MHz, and a power level of around 96 dBm during the experiment. Temperature registration was conducted using an Optris Xi400 infrared camera, equipped with an FPA detector (17 μm Pitch), a resolution of 382×288 pixels, and an operational spectrum of (8–14 μm), paired with a USB 2.0 cable for computer connection [9].

The software used for infrared recording and data collection is Optris PIX Connect, version 3.5.3057, designed for the OS – Windows 10/11 64 Bit. Emissive stickers used to determine the emissivity factor are circular, white in color, with $\varepsilon = 0.95$ and a diameter of $\emptyset = 20$ mm. For calibrating the camera, as well as measuring and archiving room temperature during experiments, a Raspberry Pi 3B 2 GB was utilized. Temperature measurements involved the use of a thermocouple of type K (NiCr-Ni) with a range from -270 °C to $+1297$ °C. Additionally, a sensor (MAX31855 K Type Temperature Sensor SPI Converter Module 3–5 V 14-bit ESP8266) was employed. This device captures the voltage change of the type K (NiCr-Ni) thermocouple, converts it to a digital signal, and then displays the temperature with accuracy up to the second decimal place.

Both the desktop and laptop computers run on the Windows 11 64 Bit OS, facilitating data processing. For determining the parameters of a mobile network to which a mobile device is connected, the G-Mon Pro software for Android was used. For the experiments involving Wi-Fi signals, a Telecom Speedport W 724 V router was utilized. This router supports Wi-Fi frequencies of both 2.4 GHz and 5 GHz.

Before each experiment, a one-time check and calibration of the infrared camera are performed. The Raspberry Pi 3B device, in combination with the MAX31855 K converter and the attached type K thermocouple, is used for this purpose. A software, developed using the Python programming language, reads and archives the temperature from the sensor. This system has been pre-calibrated using a professional Fluke brand thermocouple calibration device - Thermoelement-Kalibrierofen 9118 A. The calibration was done by a company in May 2022. The infrared camera's check was done by taking a reference temperature from the thermocouple and comparing it to the camera's readings. Temperatures ranging from 15 °C to 125 °C were used for the comparison. The observed discrepancies were in the order of $\pm 1.31\%$, which, for the purpose of the experiments, is considered an acceptable deviation, and no additional adjustments were made.

To ascertain the precise temperature in the studied areas, emissive stickers were employed with the objective of determining the emissivity coefficient of human skin. These emissive stickers, as specified by the manufacturer, have a known emissivity coefficient (in this case, $\varepsilon = 0.95$). The sticker is affixed to the subject, and due to the conductive transfer of heat from the subject to the sticker, it becomes feasible to compare the camera's temperature readings on the sticker with those of its adjacent areas. By referencing the sticker's emissivity coefficient, the skin's coefficient can be deduced. For the purpose of comparing the derived results, the foundational emissivity coefficient for human skin, ranging between $\varepsilon = 0.95$–0.98 [6], was taken into consideration. The process of documenting the actual temperature increment and contrasting it against the baseline thermal image is intricate.

For a more lucid interpretation of the results, a program has been developed in the MATLAB environment with the following functionality: the infrared camera's data is extracted in a csv format, with each thermal image being uploaded individually. This software is capable of juxtaposing two images, essentially data from two distinct thermal imageries. Upon retrieval, the data is stored in the form of matrices composed of real numbers. Subsequently, the algorithm pinpoints the apex temperature value recorded in the initial thermal image and assesses its frequency of occurrence within the captured scene. The subsequent step is to ascertain the number of instances the same or an even elevated temperature is detected in the secondary thermal image. Grounded upon this juxtaposition, a conclusion can be drawn regarding the extent of temperature surge between the primary and secondary images.

Another function of the software is to identify the hottest point (the pixel with the highest temperature on the second image) and to display the temperature difference between the first and second thermal images. This reveals the actual degree by which the temperature has risen between the compared scenes. It should be noted that the highest temperature on all thermal images must be a part of the body of the participant in the experiment – otherwise, the data and subsequent conclusions could be compromised. Another critical stipulation is that the entire area occupied by the mobile device and the zone around it must be visible. This ensures that the analyzed data will include those of the experiment, even if significant thermo effects on the body are not detected during it. In conducting the current experiments, this factor was taken into consideration, and all thermal images were captured in a way that meets this condition. The baseline will be the hottest point from the image taken prior to the initiation of the experiment. Subsequently, one would compare how many points (pixels) from the images, taken at the end of the experiment, exhibit the same or higher temperature.

3.2 Experiments

Experiment 1: The object of this experiment is to study the temperature change in the head region during active use of a mobile phone on an LTE 4G+network for a 7-year-old boy and a 12-year-old girl. The experiment has a duration of 20 min, with the temperature being recorded at the beginning, at the 10-min mark since the start of the experiment, and immediately after its conclusion. The mobile phone is placed near the right ear. The thermographic images are presented in Fig. 2.

The measurement results have been summarized and systematized in Table 1.

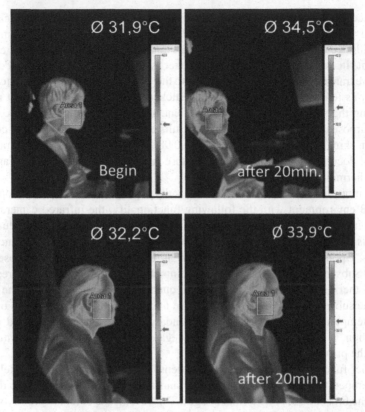

Fig. 2. Thermographic images captured at the beginning and end of the experiment (after 20 min) during the utilization of LTE+800 MHz

Upon comparing the outcomes of the conducted experiments, a more pronounced temperature increase is observed in the active region of the head in male participants under identical conditions. This can be attributed to males having a higher water content in their tissues. It is essential to recognize the influence of the body's protective mechanisms during a temperature rise, bearing in mind that each organism may exhibit distinct reactions under similar circumstances [12–14]. The comparative analysis of the presented data leads to the conclusion that in all the studies, the most significant temperature escalation occurs within the first 10–15 min, after which this warming trend decreases. In all experiments, there is no detected increase in temperature on the opposite side of the head, indicating that the warming effect is localized only to the body region near the Electromagnetic Field (EMF) source. After the termination of the experiment, the warming effect diminishes relatively swiftly.

Experiment 2: The aim of this experiment is to investigate the temperature variations in the head region of children during active use of a mobile phone connected to a private Wi-Fi network. The subjects for this study remain consistent with those from the

Table 1. Results of temperature measurements on the head during the usage of a mobile phone connected to an LTE 4G+network

	Male	Female
Begin		
The average temperature in the marked region at the beginning of the experiment	31.9 °C	32.2 °C
Maximum recorded temperature	36.4 °C	36.2 °C
The 20th minute of the experiment		
Number of pixels with this temperature equal to or greater than the average temperature at the beginning of the experiment	313	76
Maximum temperature measured at the end of the experiment	37.5 °C	36.9 °C
Change in the average temperature of the head	1.1 °C	0.7 °C
Average temperature in the marked area at the end of the experiment	34.5 °C	33.9 °C

previous experiment to ensure data comparability. The same mobile device, Huawei P30-G, was employed, with the working frequency of the signal during the experiment being approximately 5.18 GHz and a power around 72 dBm. The duration of the experiment was set at 20 min, with temperature readings taken initially and subsequently every 5 min until the conclusion of the experiment. The mobile phone was positioned near the right ear. Thermographic images from the experiment can be found in Fig. 3.

The measurement results have been summarized and systematized in Table 2.

As observed from the thermographic images, the increase in temperature in the male participant is again more pronounced compared to the female participant under equal conditions. In this case, due to the higher frequency of the signal, the temperature rise is relatively less compared to the experiment with the LTE+4G network. This is attributed to the fact that higher frequency EM waves carry relatively lower energy, which restricts their ability to penetrate deep into soft tissues and induce significant and prolonged heating in the active area. This is further supported by the finding that the heating effect diminishes more rapidly after the experiment, compared to the previous experiment.

During the experiment, the most significant temperature increase was observed within the initial 15 min. Following this period, the male participant exhibited virtually no discernible temperature difference. Conversely, the female participant demonstrated a slight decrease in the temperature profile during the final 5 min of the experiment.

Despite the milder warming effect when using a mobile network of a higher frequency, the thermal effect is evident. This effect could pose potential health risks not only to children but also to adults.

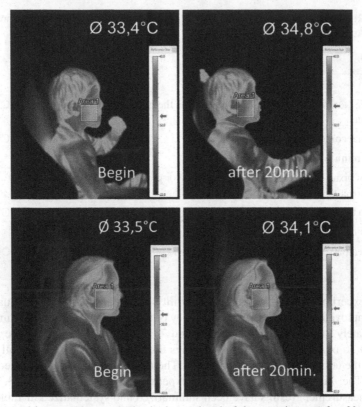

Fig. 3. Thermal images taken at the beginning and end of the experiment (after 20 min) using Wi-Fi 5, 18 GHz

Table 2. Results of temperature measurements on the head during the use of a mobile phone connected to a private Wi-Fi network

	Male	Female
Begin		
The average temperature in the marked region at the beginning of the experiment	33.4 °C	33.5 °C
Maximum recorded temperature	37.0 °C	36.5 °C
The 20th minute of the experiment		
Number of pixels with this temperature equal to or greater than the average temperature at the beginning of the experiment	78	18
Maximum temperature measured at the end of the experiment	37.6 °C	36.9 °C
Change in the average temperature of the head	0.6 °C	0.4 °C
Average temperature in the marked area at the end of the experiment	33.5 °C	34.1 °C

4   Conclusion

During the conduct of the current experiments, precautions were taken to minimize extraneous electromagnetic (EM) interference, such as from other Wi-Fi networks or wireless devices emitting electromagnetic radiation (EMR). Furthermore, the same device with a specified Specific Absorption Rate (SAR) was consistently utilized. The presence of additional EM interference, particularly in residential buildings or multi-family homes, and the use of devices with a higher SAR coefficient can amplify the warming effect on humans.

The conducted experiments conclusively support the hypothesis that modern mobile phones and their prolonged use can exert a physical effect on the human body in the form of warming, induced by the device's electromagnetic field. It is essential to consider the higher water content in children's tissues, which in turn intensifies this warming effect. Most experts' recommendations related to mobile phone usage include limiting call durations, reducing the EMR power by increasing the distance between the GSM device and the human body, even when the phone is not in call mode.

Acknowledgement. This work is supported by the Bulgarian National Science Fund, project title "Synthesis of a dynamic model for assessing the psychological and physical impacts of excessive use of smart technologies", KP-06-N 32/4/07.12.2019. We extend our profound gratitude to Optris GmbH, Berlin for their invaluable provision of equipment, instrumental in the execution of the conducted experiments.

References

1. Garvanova, M.: Effects of Excessive Use of Smart Technologies on Human. Data Processing from Empirical and Experimental Research, p. 260. Academic Publisher "Za bukvite – O pismeneh, Monograph, Sofia (2022)
2. Garvanov, I., Jotsov, V., Garvanova, M.: Data science modeling for EEG signal filtering using wavelet transforms. In: Proceedings of 2020 IEEE 10th International Conference on Intelligent Systems (IS), 28–30 August 2020, Varna, Bulgaria, pp. 352–357 (2020). https://doi.org/10.1109/IS48319.2020.9199843
3. Garvanova, M., Garvanov, I., Borissova, D.: The influence of electromagnetic fields on human brain. In: Proceedings of the XXI International Symposium on Electrical Apparatus and Technologies (SIELA 2020), 3–6 June 2020, Bourgas, Bulgaria, pp. 111–114 (2020). https://doi.org/10.1109/SIELA49118.2020.9167099
4. Mobilfunk und Gesundheit. Fakten und Informationen zu Technik, Forschung und Sicherheit (2022). https://www.telekom.com/resource/blob/485028/66784fd16413f37934103de0ad087ef3/dl-fakten-mobilfunk-und-gesundheit-data.pdf
5. Chiaraviglio, L., Elzanaty, A., Alouini, M.-S.: Health risks associated with 5G exposure: a view from the communications engineering perspective. IEEE Open J. Commun. Soc. **2**, 2131–2179 (2021). https://doi.org/10.1109/OJCOMS.2021.3106052
6. Wissenschaftlicher Dienst des Europäischen Parlaments. Auswirkungen der drahtlosen 5G Kommunikation auf die menschliche Gesundheit, Brüssel: Europäische Parlament (2020)
7. Starlink-Spezifikationen (2022). https://www.starlink.com/legal/documents/DOC-1002-69942-69?regionCode=DE

8. Grüner, D.I.: Grundlagen der Berührungslosen Temperaturmessung "Strahlungsthermome-trie." Raytek GmbH, Berlin (2003)
9. Optris GmbH. Grundlagen der Brühruhgslosen Temperaturmessung, Berlin (2022)
10. Garvanova, M., Shishkov, B., Vladimirov, S.: Mobile devices–effect on human health. In: Shishkov, B. (ed.) Proceedings of the Seventh International Conference on Telecommunications and Remote Sensing–ICTRS 2018, Barcelona, Spain, pp. 101–104 (2018). https://doi.org/10.1145/3278161.3278176
11. Garvanova, M., Garvanov, I., Jotsov, V.: Data science modeling and constraint-based data selection for EEG signals denoising using wavelet transforms. In: Sgurev, V., Jotsov, V., Kacprzyk, J. (eds.) Advances in Intelligent Systems Research and Innovation. SSDC, vol. 379, pp. 241–267. Springer, Cham (2022). https://doi.org/10.1007/978-3-030-78124-8_11
12. Tsonkov, G., Garvanova, M., Garvanov, I.: A study of thermal effects on humans resulting from prolonged use of a mobile phone. In: Proceedings of the VII International Scientific Conference "Industry 4.0"–Winter Session, 7–10 December 2022, Borovets, Bulgaria, vol. 4/17, pp. 281–284 (2022)
13. Pew Research Center. Parenting Children in the Age of Screens, 28 July 2020. https://www.pewresearch.org/internet/2020/07/28/parenting-children-in-the-age-of-screens/
14. Garvanova, M., et al.: A data-science approach for creation of a comprehensive model to assess the impact of mobile technologies on humans. Appl. Sci. 13(6), 3600 (2023). https://doi.org/10.3390/app13063600

Vibrations in Ships and Crew Health

Kolyo Oreshkov, Radoslav Simionov, Kamen Seymenliyski[⊠], Radostin Dolchinkov,
Silvia Letskovska, and Eldar Zaerov

Faculty of Computer Science and Engineering, Burgas Free University, Burgas, Bulgaria
kolyooreshkov@abv.bg, {kdimitrov,rado,silvia}@bfu.bg

Abstract. The machinery compartment of the ship is one of the key components
ensuring the proper functioning of the ship's engine and, consequently, the operation of the entire vessel. The crew responsible for the machinery compartment
is exposed to various factors that can influence their health and safety. One of
these factors is vibrations generated by the operating machinery and equipment.
The aim of this study is to investigate the impact of vibrations in the machinery
compartment of a ship on the health and safety of the crew. Potential health issues
related to vibrations will be analyzed, and measures to reduce the risk to the crew
will be examined.

Keywords: Machinery compartment · Vibrations · Crew health and safety ·
Measures to reduce risk

1 Introduction

Maritime transportation is pivotal for global trade, with the vast majority of goods chan-
neled via sea. Within this intricate system, the machinery compartment is paramount,
facilitating the operation of ships' engines. As ships become technologically advanced,
their machinery compartments, while exhibiting engineering prowess, also introduce
health and safety challenges for the crew.

Prominent among these challenges are vibrations, generated by operational machinery. Over time, even subtle vibrations can precipitate health risks. Prior research affirms
the adverse health effects stemming from sustained exposure to specific vibration frequencies (Smith et al., 2019; Jensen & Møller, 2017). Beyond individual health ramifications, vibrations can compromise crew efficiency, potentially imperiling maritime
safety due to operational oversights (Williams, 2018).

This study aims to thoroughly assess the machinery compartment vibrations' reper-
cussions on crew health and safety. By harnessing robust methodologies and leveraging
empirical data, the research aspires to deepen our grasp on this issue, steering the maritime industry towards enhanced strategies that prioritize crew well-being and bolster
operational integrity [1–3].

© The Author(s), under exclusive license to Springer Nature Switzerland AG 2023
B. Shishkov and A. Lazarov (Eds.): ICTRS 2023, CCIS 1990, pp. 127–135, 2023.
https://doi.org/10.1007/978-3-031-49263-1_10

2   Measurements and Standards

2.1   Methods of Vibration Measurement

Accelerometers: Accelerometers are devices used to measure the acceleration transmitted through various points in the machinery compartment. Measurements can be taken at both static and dynamic points to determine vibration levels. Spectral Analysis: Spectral analysis can be employed to study the frequency content of vibrations. This allows the identification of frequency ranges that are relevant to the health and safety of the crew. Long-term Measurements: Long-term measurements can provide a comprehensive understanding of vibrations in the machinery compartment. These may include periodic or continuous recordings of vibration levels over an extended period.

Measurement Units:

- Acceleration: Acceleration is measured in meters per square second (m/s^2) or gravitational forces (g).
- Force: Force is measured in newtons (N).
- Velocity: Velocity is measured in meters per second (m/s) or, in some cases, rotating components in revolutions per minute (RPM).
- Deformation: Deformation is measured in percentages (%).

It is essential to note that the methods of investigation and measurement units may vary depending on the specific study and available resources. During the literature review, it will be useful to explore various articles that provide information on the methods and measurement units used in previous research [4–6].

Vibration measurements should be conducted under different conditions and time periods to obtain an understanding of the vibration levels to which the crew is exposed in various operational scenarios. These measurements can be compared to regulatory standards and guidelines that define safe vibration levels in ship machinery compartments.

2.2   International Standards

International standards regarding ship vibrations delineate measurement techniques, limits, and assessment criteria. A prominent standard is ISO 6954:2000, detailing methods to measure vibrations from marine internal combustion engines on ships' fixed structures. Another is ISO 20283-1:2016, defining assessment methods for workers' health exposure to these vibrations. Additional standards include ISO 20283-2:2016, which targets vibrations in small ships; ISO 6955:2001, focusing on ship deck vibrations; and ISO 20283-3:2016, evaluating vibrations' effects on ship accommodation and workspaces. ISO's intent with these standards is a universally recognized approach to evaluating ship vibrations and their influence on personnel. The IMO's MSC/Circ. 685 offers guidelines for assessing ship vibrations, while MSC/Circ. 908 and MSC/Circ. 1175 provide guidance on vibrations from defective propulsion systems and propellers, respectively.

3   Crew Health Status Analysis

Analyzing the crew's health is pivotal in studying the effects of engine room vibrations on their well-being and safety. The report's third section uses a survey to glean direct feedback from crew members about health symptoms tied to their engine room duties. Here's a condensed outline:

- Survey Design: A structured survey will probe into health symptoms linked to engine room tasks, like headaches, skin issues, fatigue, balance problems, etc.
- Distribution: Targeting all engine room crew members, the survey can be shared through e-forms, hard copies, or online platforms.
- Data Compilation: Post-collection, data undergoes statistical analyses like correlation studies and descriptive statistics.
- Results Analysis: Insights drawn from data will focus on symptom frequency, severity, and the possible association with engine room tasks.

Incorporating further details:

- Result Assessment: Survey outcomes will be gauged against existing health norms, possibly benchmarking against stipulated vibration impact standards.
- Risk Factor Identification: Analyzing data can spotlight potential risks linking vibrations to health symptoms, possibly zeroing in on specific machinery as culprits.
- Correlation Exploration: Delving deeper, one can discern which vibration frequencies or amplitudes correlate strongest with health complaints.
- Mitigation Measures: Informed by health data, steps like machinery isolation, innovative work methods, or shock-absorption solutions can be deployed.
- Periodic Re-evaluation: Regularly repeating this health check ensures ongoing monitoring, assessing vibration-reducing measure effectiveness.

Ultimately, understanding the nexus between engine room vibrations and crew health equips stakeholders to better the working milieu and safety. Such initiatives not only safeguard crew health but also elevate the technical efficiency aboard vessels [7, 8].

4   Standardized Practical Investigation in a Real Work Environment

The practical investigation applies the following definitions and standards:

- Hand-Arm Vibration: The mechanical vibration transmitted to the hand-arm, which leads to risks to health and safety, especially for workers, including vascular, skeletal, joint, neurological, or muscular disorders.
- Whole-Body Vibration: The mechanical vibration transmitted to the whole body, leading to risks to health and safety for workers, particularly specific conditions in the lower back and spinal column injuries.
- Daily Exposure to Hand-Arm Vibration (ms^{-2}): The time-weighted average of accelerations measured over a nominal eight-hour working day.
- Daily Exposure to Whole-Body Vibration (ms^{-2}): The time-averaged, weighted acceleration values measured over a nominal eight-hour working day.

Legislative Decree No. 81/2008 defines exposure limit values and corresponding actions as follows:

• Exposure Limit Value (ELV): The exposure level whose exceeding is prohibited and must be prevented as it includes an unacceptable risk for the exposed subject in the absence of protective equipment. • Action Value (AV): The exposure level from which specific protective measures for the exposed individuals must be implemented.

Article 201, paragraph 1 of Legislative Decree No. 81/2008 establishes the following exposure limit (Table 1):

Table 1. Standards for Action Values and Exposure Limit Values

Definition	Hand-Arm Vibration	Whole-Body Vibration
Action Value (AV)	2.5 m/s^2	0.5 m/s^2
Exposure Limit Value (ELV)	5.0 m/s^2	1.0 m/s^2

The relevant passage in Article 201, paragraph 2, states: "In cases where there is a change in the level of daily exposure, the maximum daily level should be used." Therefore, this applies to exposure that occurs routinely rather than exceptional cases.

4.1 Short Periods of Exposure

The Law on Health and Safety Conditions at Work introduces what is known as exposure for short periods, and the decree does not actually specify quantitative values. The following table summarizes the levels of exposure for short periods (Table 2).

Table 2. Standards for short exposure periods.

Definition	Hand-Arm Vibration	Whole-Body Vibration
Short Periods of Exposure	20 m/s^2	1.5 m/s^2

The daily exposure calculated for the main ship positions was compared to legal limits to determine the level of risk faced by the worker. Three risk classes have been defined, each assigned a color code for easy identification. The following tables summarize the legal restrictions, risk classes, and an overview of actions to be taken (Tables 3, 4, and 5):

Table 3. Risk Classes

Class	Hand-Arm Vibration	Whole Body Vibration
Class 0	Daily Exposure < 2.5 m/s^2	Daily Exposure < 0.5m/s^2
Class 1	2.5 m/s$^2 <$ Daily Exposure < 5 m/s^2	0.5 m/s$^2 <$ Daily Exposure < 1.0 m/s^2
Class 2	Daily Exposure < 5 m/s^2	Daily Exposure > 1.0 m/s^2

Table 4. Description of Risk Classes.

Class	Risk	Induced acceleration intensity
Class 0	Low	… Lower than the action value
Class 1	Medium	… Between the action value and the exposure limit value
Class 2	High	… Higher than the exposure limit value

Table 5. Actions by the employer.

Class	Risk	Actions by the employer
Class 0	Low	No action is required
Class 1	Medium	The employer must take measures to reduce exposure levels below the action value
Class 2	High	The employer must take measures to reduce exposure levels below the action value The employer must take immediate actions to reduce the exposure, identify why the limitations have been exceeded, and take measures for prevention and protection against their future exceedance

4.2 Methods and Instruments Used in Measurements

The measurements were conducted based on the individual's position on the ship and their specific job specification, whether it was primarily physical or administrative, their workplace on the ship, and their physical position during execution.

The most frequently visited work areas of the personnel were measured using triaxial accelerometers. Additionally, most workstations and hand-held tools were also measured. Measurement instruments are calibrated at least every two years in an accredited calibration laboratory.

A portion of the measurements is presented in Tables 6 and 7:

Table 6. Measurements of vibrations (hand and body) on ship job positions.

Job position on the ship	Hand-Arm Vibration	Whole Body Vibration
Captain	–	0.12
Staff-Captain	–	0.12
1st Bridge Officer	–	0.12
2nd Bridge Officer	–	0.12
3rd Bridge Officer	–	0.12
Fire-fighting Safety Officer	–	0.11
Environmental Officer	–	0.12
Boatswain	2.05	0.16
Ordinary seaman	2.10	0.17
Security Officer	–	0.12
Chief Engineer	–	0.14
Chief Electrical Engineer	1.0	0.15
Electrician	1.1	0.20
1st Engineer	1.1	0.22
2nd Engineer	1.4	0.21
3rd Engineer	1.2	0.21
Storekeeper	1.5	0.18
Motorman	1.4	0.24
Wiper (engine room)	1.5	0.23

Table 7. Workplace Vibration Measurements.

Working area/Service area	On the x-axis (awx)	Whole body vibration, on the y-axis (awy)	On the z-axis (awz)
Engine Control Room	0.03	0.02	0.01
Generator 1	0.07	0.08	0.09
Generator 2	0.07	0.08	0.08
Generator 3	0.08	0.1	0.09
Generator 4	0.03	0.09	0.06
Emergency Generator	0.06	0.06	0.07
Boiler	0.01	0.03	0.02

(*continued*)

Table 7. (*continued*)

Working area/Service area	On the x-axis (awx)	Whole body vibration, on the y-axis (awy)	On the z-axis (awz)
Lub-Oil Separator 1	0.09	0.09	0.09
Lub-Oil Separator 2	0.08	0.09	0.08
MDO-Separator 1	0.07	0.08	0.07
MDO-Separator 2	0.06	0.08	0.07
MDO-Separator 3	0.08	0.09	0.09
Engine Store 1	0.04	0.04	0.04
Engine Store 2	0.03	0.04	0.03
Evaporator 1	0.02	0.09	0.06

5 Recommendations and Measures for Risk Reduction

Reducing adverse effects of vibrations on a ship's crew is paramount. Based on the vibration study, the following condensed recommendations are offered to address this:

1. **Equipment Optimization**:

   - Collaborate with manufacturers to improve machinery design for vibration reduction.
   - Implement balancing devices, ensuring regular maintenance.

2. **Vibration Isolation**:

   - Install vibration isolators designed per ship needs, and use dampers and vibration-absorbing plates on affected areas.

3. **Crew Training and Awareness**:

   - Train crew on symptom recognition, equipment handling, and protective gear usage.
   - Inform about relevant vibration and health regulations.

4. **Technology and Method Development**:

   - Engage in research for innovative vibration reduction techniques, including active vibration control systems.

5. **Regular Maintenance and Inspections**:

   - Ensure routine equipment checks and replace malfunctioning components.

6. **Work Process Modifications**:

   - Distribute work, rotate crew schedules, and implement regular rest periods to minimize exposure.

7. **Use of PPE**:

- Provide crew with vibration-reducing gloves, footwear, and other equipment.

8. **Procedures and Protocols**:

- Develop comprehensive protocols for work in the engine room and a reporting mechanism for issues.

9. **Vibration Control at Source**:

- Incorporate vibration-absorbing materials within equipment and reevaluate system designs.

10. **Vibration Transmission Path Control**:

- Minimize vibration transfer with specialized isolation materials and structures.

Adhering to these recommendations, aligned with evolving standards and technologies, will foster enhanced working conditions and crew safety.

6 Conclusions

The study of the impact of vibrations in the ship's engine room on the health and safety of the crew is essential for protecting crew health and ensuring the proper functioning of the crew. The results of the study will contribute to the development of appropriate measures and recommendations for reducing risk and improving working conditions in the ship's engine room.

References

1. Jensen, A., Jepsen, J.R.: Vibration on board and health effects. Int. Maritime Health 64(2):66–68 (2014). https://doi.org/10.5603/IMH.2014.0013
2. Carter, T., Jepsen, J.: Exposures and health effects at sea: report on the NIVA course: maritime occupational medicine, exposures and health effects at Sea Elsinore, Denmark. Med. Int. Maritime Health (2014)
3. Pazara, T., Pricop, M., Novac, G., Pricop, C.: The application of new noise and vibration standards on board ships. In: 4th International Scientific Conference SEA-CONF 2018, IOP Conference Series: Earth and Environmental Science, vol. 172, p. 012027 (2018). https://doi.org/10.1088/1755-1315/172/1/012027
4. Dev, A., Chia, R., Tam, I.: Maritime sustainability and maritime labour convention - reducing vibration and noise levels on board ships for health and safety of seafarers. Conference: MARTECH 2017 SINGAPORE; Towards 2030: Maritime Sustainability through People and TechnologyAt: Singapore (2017)
5. Olausson, K.: On Evaluation and Modelling of Human Exposure to Vibration and Shockon Planing High-Speed Craft, Academic thesis with permission by KTH Royal Institute of Technology, Stockholm, to be submitted for public examination for the degree of Licentiate in Vehicle and Maritime Engineering, Thursday the 12th of February, 2015 at 10.00, in D3, Lindstedtsvägen 5, KTH-Royal Institute of Technology, Stockholm, Sweden. TRITA-AVE2015:01 ISSN1651-7660

6. Matsankov, M., Ivanova, M.: Selection of optimal variant of hybrid system under conditions of uncertainty. In: The 2nd International Conference on Electrical Engineering and Green Energy, Roma, 28–30 June 2019. E3S Web Conf. **115**, 01007 (2019). https://www.e3s-conferences.org/articles/e3sconf/abs/2019/41/contents/contents.html
7. Obretenov, D., Simeon Iliev, S.: Prospects for the development of internal combustion engines. In: Proceedings of University of Ruse, vol. 60 (2021). Book 4.3 FRI-2.209-1-TMS-05:25-29
8. Matsankov, M., Petrov, S.: Modeling of the induced voltage in a disconnected grounded conductor of a three-phase power line. Int. Conf. Smart City Green Energy (ICSCGE) **2021**, 75–78 (2021). https://doi.org/10.1109/ICSCGE53744.2021.9654332

A Review of Pilotless Vehicles

Boris Shishkov[1,2,3](✉) and Gabriela Garvanova[2,4]

[1] Institute of Mathematics and Informatics, Bulgarian Academy of Sciences, Sofia, Bulgaria
`b.b.shishkov@iicrest.org`
[2] Faculty of Information Sciences, University of Library Studies and Information Technologies,
Sofia, Bulgaria
`gabigarvanova@abv.bg`
[3] Institute IICREST, Sofia, Bulgaria
[4] Institute of Information and Communication Technologies, Bulgarian Academy of Sciences,
Sofia, Bulgaria

Abstract. We have been enjoying different modes of transport for many decades already, including road transport, water transport, and air transport. Further reflections of this are the pilotless forms, such as autonomous cars, unmanned water/underwater vehicles, unmanned aerial vehicles, and so on. Even though they are diverse conceptually and technologically, we argue that there are common current challenges characterizing all pilotless vehicles: (i) Standardization is not yet adequate and exhaustive; (ii) The current rules and legislation are insufficiently capable of properly regulating the use of such vehicles; (iii) Accountability is an issue and hence it is not straightforward to identify who is responsible in case of an accident. As a result: pilotless vehicles are not widely used and deployed, authorities are not capable of fully regulating their use, insurance companies have no corresponding products, and so on. Addressing this problem, we provide a brief review of pilotless vehicles from a user perspective, as a step forward in better understanding and utilizing them.

Keywords: Information and Communication Technology (ICT) · Pilotless vehicles

1 Introduction

We have studied the technical and technological progress over the years, aligning this to the developments in ICT (Information and Communication Technology) – all this affecting transport as well [1]. We have been enjoying different modes of transport for many decades already, including road transport, water transport, and air transport [2]. Nevertheless, the needs for even better coverage and availability as well as the increasing labor costs have inspired ICT-enabled developments towards pilotless vehicles [3]. Expectations used to be high also in other aspects, such as the necessity to approach disruptive events in more safe and more effective ways, keeping the human agents in the distance [4].

© The Author(s), under exclusive license to Springer Nature Switzerland AG 2023
B. Shishkov and A. Lazarov (Eds.): ICTRS 2023, CCIS 1990, pp. 136–143, 2023.
https://doi.org/10.1007/978-3-031-49263-1_11

We have seen drones, fulfilling missions in the sky [5], we have seen autonomous cars [6], we have seen pilotless underwater vehicles [7], and so on.

Even though they are diverse conceptually and technologically, we argue that there are common current challenges characterizing all pilotless vehicles:

- Standardization is not yet adequate and exhaustive – we miss exhaustive safety standards, exhaustive reliability standards, coverage of accident "patterns", and so on [8];
- The current rules and legislation are insufficiently capable of properly regulating the use of such vehicles [9];
- As we have studied in previous work, accountability is an issue and for this reason it is not straightforward to identify who is responsible in case of an accident [10].

Hence, pilotless vehicles are not widely used and deployed, authorities are not capable of fully regulating their use, insurance companies have no corresponding products, and so on.

Addressing this problem, we briefly review and discuss pilotless vehicles from a user perspective, as a step forward in better understanding and utilizing them. Since we are reporting research-in-progress, we are not offering validation as it concerns our discussion and claims – we plan this for future research.

The remainder of the current paper is organized as follows: A brief state-of-the-art analysis follows in Sect. 2. Section 3 discusses different aspects concerning pilotless vehicles from a user perspective. Finally, Sect. 4 provides the conclusions.

2 Background

With regard to the remainder of the paper, we consider references as follows:

- Concerning drones: [11–25];
- Pilotless (under)-water vehicles: [26–32];
- Autonomous cars: [33–39].

An Unmanned Aerial Vehicle (UAV), commonly known as a DRONE, is an aircraft without any human pilot, crew, or passengers on board. UAVs were originally developed through the twentieth century for military missions and by the twenty-first, they had become essential assets to most militaries as reconnaissance, armed attacks, military training and many others. Drones are used across the world not only for military applications but also for civilian purposes. The use of UAVs has grown rapidly in recent years because, unlike manned aircraft, they are cheap, can stay in the air for many hours, and find more and more practical applications. Drones are very different depending on their technical characteristics and way of implementation. Next to drones that are AERIAL, we also have pilotless vehicles that concern LAND ("autonomous cars" have a passenger on board) and WATER (referred to as "pilotless (under)-water vehicles"). Drones seem to be currently most popular as well as autonomous cars. UAVs can be classified by the technology of flying, material of construction, method of control, foot load capacity, height and length of flight and many others.

With low production costs, the use of drones has expanded to many non-military applications, such as: remote sensing, aerial photography, precision agriculture, forest fire detection and monitoring, newsgathering, crowd surveillance, disaster management, and so on. Police and authorities are using drones for surveillance, maritime patrol, border patrol missions, delivery of medicines to inaccessible regions, coordination of humanitarian aid, and so on.

Aerial surveillance of large areas include environmental monitoring, illegal land-fill detection, river monitoring, livestock monitoring, counting wildlife and detection of illegal hunting, wildfire mapping, archaeology, oil, gas and mineral exploration and production, pipeline security, home security, search and rescue, road patrol and antipiracy. UAVs can be used to perform geophysical surveys, in particular geomagnetic surveys where measurements of the Earth's varying magnetic field strength are used to calculate the nature of the underlying magnetic rock structure. A knowledge of the underlying rock structure helps to predict the location of mineral deposits. UAVs equipped with air quality monitors provide real-time air analysis at various elevations. Hence, UAVs are particularly useful when accessing areas that are dangerous for manned aircraft.

Civil uses include inspection of power lines and/or pipelines, landslide measurement, illegal landfill detection, and so on. Further, UAVs are particularly useful for roof inspections, wind turbine inspections, mining inspections and others that can be dangerous for Humans to realize. Finally, equipped with thermal cameras, drones can be useful for solar panel and/or building inspections.

As it concerns agriculture, farmers use UAVs to spray crops – that is cheaper than using helicopters, for example. Next to that, drones can be used in monitoring as it concerns livestock, crops and water levels.

And in the end, UAVs can be used in approaching fires, in investigating accidents, in fighting smuggling, in (pilot) trainings, and in entertainment.

3 Discussion

As mentioned in the Introduction, the current section discusses different aspects concerning pilotless vehicles, taking a user perspective. Further, we limit the discussion to consider just three vehicle items, namely: AUTONOMOUS CAR (relevant to LAND transportation), DRONE (relevant to AIR transportation), and PILOTLESS UNDER-WATER VEHICLE (relevant to WATER transportation). In this we not only cover the three main transportation modes but we also take into account that the abovementioned items are most widely used to date. Finally, we carry out the discussion, following three essential user-perspective-related directions, namely the usability mode itself (where the vehicle USER is in the focus), regulations (where corresponding SOCIETAL concerns are in the focus), and APPLICABILITY (where the FUNCTIONAL benefit from the vehicle is in the focus). For the sake of brevity, we are just mentioning several key issues in this section, part of the current position paper, leaving it for future work to go in more detail along those lines.

3.1 Usability Mode

We argue that drones and pilotless underwater vehicles are quite similar as it concerns usability mode; for this reason, in the current sub-section, we consider drones vs. autonomous cars.

A drone performs a mission in the sky with no passengers on board. Splitting decision-making and control is two-fold: (i) Supported by its own sensors and other data sources, the drone itself generates useful (contextual) information that is used by corresponding drone modules (comprising hardware and software) for generating "conclusions" that in turn maintain control and support decision-making; (ii) This goes in combination with instructions from the ground (that are based on mission-related and/or contextual information) where people are expected to be active in support with the drone mission. In case of tensions between (i) and (ii), usually ground commands would prevail. And then we come to the question "Who is the User?" Actually, determining the primary user concerning a drone mission is not always straightforward – if this is a land-border-related mission, the primary users would be the border police officers servicing the particular land border area (they need monitoring data generated by the drone, used in support of the need to adequately determine the "current" situation); if this is a rescue operation, then the primary user would be the person(s) being rescued; if this is about getting photos of somewhere, then the primary user would be the one who needs those photos; if this is about pollution-related monitoring, then the primary user would be Society in whose interest environment is monitored; and so on.

An autonomous car is transporting a person from Point A to Point B – hence, the only PRIMARY user is the person being transported. Furthering this line of reasoning would come to the point that logically the INTEREST of the primary user should be reaching Point B as fast as possible. In this regard, it is to be mentioned that ALWAYS there are SECONDARY users as it concerns autonomous cars: pedestrians, cyclists and others would need safety for themselves while Society would need the autonomous car to "behave" adequately in the particular city or region. This may lead to delays that in turn is "conflicting" as it concerns the interest of the primary user. In approaching this, the interest of the primary user should be fulfilled in the best possible way but RESTRICTED by the NEED to not hurt ESSENTIAL interests of other stakeholders and/or Society.

For the sake of exhaustiveness, it is to be mentioned that often such "secondary" interests may need to be taken into account in drone missions as well, and then they are to be considered in a similar way as mentioned above.

Still, the main difference between autonomous cars and drones, as it concerns the usability mode is that the PRIMARY user of an autonomous car can only be the person being transported while the PRIMARY user as it concerns a drone mission is not always so straightforward to determine.

3.2 Regulations

Autonomous cars are FORCED to conform to all rules and regulations governing auto-traffic in general and big drones that are flying at high altitudes are FORCED to conform to all rules and regulations governing air traffic. In contrast, small drones (flying at low altitudes) and pilotless underwater vehicles are "sneaking" in, in a "room" with no consistent and exhaustive legislation, globally harmonized. For this reason, often small drones and pilotless underwater vehicles de facto are governed by no rules. In our view this can be dangerous because such vehicles could:

- Hurt somebody (imagine that a drone falls upon the head of a person);
- Violate public values (imagine that a drone photographs the face of a person against the will of the person);
- Transport hazardous goods (imagine that a pilotless underwater vehicle carries explosives on board that leads to the damage of a yacht that appears to be several meters above the vehicle);
- and so on.

Hence, changes in global legislation are needed to address those issues.

At the same time, there are ACCOUNTABILITY-related concerns that stay not only for small drones and pilotless underwater vehicles but also for other drones and pilotless cars – sometimes it would be difficult to establish who is RESPONSIBLE in case of an accident/damage. We have studied this, addressing particularly drones [10] but those concerns are to be considered in a broader way. We argue that among the solution directions in this regard should be providing adequate TRACEABILITY in the software servicing the vehicle modules.

3.3 Applicability

As it concerns autonomous cars, they essentially serve for transporting the person on board while the applicability of drones is much broader, as we have already discussed in the previous sections of the current paper, and it is similar as it concerns pilotless underwater vehicles. Hence, not claiming exhaustiveness, and not considering autonomous cars, we outline several key application directions characterizing both drones and pilotless underwater vehicles:

- Monitoring;
- Rescue operations;
- Transportation of goods.

Again, this list is not considered exhaustive, just we claim that those three application directions are essential as it concerns unmanned aerial (under)-water vehicles.

4   Conclusions

In this paper, we have considered pilotless vehicles, paying special attention to drones as well as autonomous cars and pilotless underwater vehicles. Acknowledging relevant challenges, such as lack of adequate standardization and regulations as well as accountability-related issues, we observe that those are hampering the full-value deployment, utilization, and use of pilotless vehicles. Addressing this problem, we have briefly reviewed and discussed them from a user perspective.

Since we are reporting research-in-progress, we have not offered validation as it concerns our discussion and claims.

In future research, we plan to: (a) Further partition this work to explicitly distinguish among land pilotless vehicles, aerial ones, and (under)water ones, for the sake of identifying similarities, differences, and crosscutting concerns, from the perspective of usability; (b) Consider examples for the sake of (partially) justifying our claims; (c)

Reflect our realized literature studies in a systematic literature review; (d) Consider also other public values [1] next to accountability, such as safety, privacy, and so on.

Acknowledgement. This work was supported by the National Science Program "Security and Defense", which has received funding from the Ministry of Education and Science of the Republic of Bulgaria under the grant agreement № D01-74/19.05.2022.

References

1. Shishkov, B.: Designing Enterprise Information Systems, Merging Enterprise Modeling and Software Specification. Springer, Cham (2020)
2. Rakkesh, S.T., Weerasinghe, A.R., Ranasinghe, R.A.C.:Effective urban transport planning using multi-modal traffic simulations approach. In: 2016 Moratuwa Engineering Research Conference (MERCon), Moratuwa, pp. 303–308 (2016)
3. Bandyopadhyay, A., Raj, N.S.S., Varghese, J.T.: Coexisting in a world with urban air mobility: a revolutionary transportation system. In: 2018 Advances in Science and Engineering Technology International Conferences (ASET), Dubai, Sharjah, pp. 1–6 (2018)
4. Shishkov, B., Verbraeck, A.: Making enterprise information systems resilient against disruptive events: a conceptual view. In: Shishkov, B. (eds.) Business Modeling and Software Design. BMSD 2020. Lecture Notes in Business Information Processing, vol. 391. Springer, Cham (2020)
5. IEEE Draft Standard for Drone Applications Framework. In: P1936.1, 2020, pp. 1–29 (Feb 2021)
6. Baajaruddin, N.C., Baki, K.A., Suhendar: Autonomous car based on teaching-and-playback control. In: 2020 International Conference on Applied Science and Technology (iCAST), Padang, pp. 657–661 (2020)
7. Yar, G.N.A.H., Ahmad, A., Khurshid, K.: Low cost assembly design of unmanned underwater vehicle (UUV). In: International Bhurban Conference on Applied Sciences and Technologies (IBCAST), pp. 829–834. IEEE (2021)
8. Fotouhi, A., et al.: Survey on UAV cellular communications: practical aspects, standardization advancements, regulation, and security challenges. In: IEEE Communications Surveys and Tutorials, vol. 21, no. 4, pp. 3417–3442, Fourthquarter (2019)
9. Xu, C., Liao, X., Tan, J., Ye, H., Lu, H.: Recent research progress of unmanned aerial vehicle regulation policies and technologies in urban low altitude. IEEE Access **8**, 74175–74194 (2020)
10. Shishkov, B., Hristozov, S., Janssen, M., Van den Hoven, J.: Drones in land border missions: benefits and accountability concerns. In: Proceedings of the 6th International Conference on Telecommunications and Remote Sensing (ICTRS 2017). ACM, New York (2017)
11. Sandbrook, C.: The social implications of using drones for biodiversity conservation. Ambio **44**(Suppl 4), 636–647 (2015)
12. Shishkov, B., Ivanova, K., Verbraeck, A., Van Sinderen, M.: Combining context-awareness and data analytics in support of drone technology. In: Shishkov, B. (eds.) Telecommunications and Remote Sensing (ICTRS 2022). Communications in Computer and Information Science, vol. 1730. Springer, Cham (2022)
13. Griffin, G.F.: The use of unmanned aerial vehicles for disaster management. Geomatica **68**(4), 265–281 (2014)

14. Shishkov, B., Branzov, T., Ivanova, K., Verbraeck, A.: Using drones for resilience: a system of systems perspective. In: Proceedings of the 10th International Conference on Telecommunications and Remote Sensing (ICTRS 2021). Association for Computing Machinery, New York (2021)
15. Shishkov, B., Hristozov, S., Verbraeck, A.: Improving resilience using drones for effective monitoring after disruptive events. In: Proceedings of the 9th International Conference on Telecommunications and Remote Sensing (ICTRS 2020). Association for Computing Machinery, New York (2020)
16. Milas, A.S., Cracknell, A.P., Warner, T.A.: Drones – the third generation source of remote sensing data. Int. J. Remote Sens. **39**(21), 7125–7137 (2018)
17. Kayan, H., Eslampanah, R., Yeganli, F., Askar, M.: Heat leakage detection and surveillance using aerial thermography drone. In: Proceedings of the 26th Signal Processing and Communications Applications Conference (SIU) (2018)
18. Pandey, S., Barik, R.K., Gupta, S., Arthi, R.: Pandemic drone with thermal imaging and crowd monitoring system (DRISHYA). In: Tripathy, H.K., Mishra, S., Mallick, P.K., Panda, A.R. (eds.) Technical Advancements of Machine Learning in Healthcare. SCI, vol. 936, pp. 307–325. Springer, Singapore (2021). https://doi.org/10.1007/978-981-33-4698-7_15
19. Hill, A.C., Laugier, E.J., Casana, J.: Archaeological remote sensing using multi-temporal, drone-acquired thermal and near infrared (NIR) imagery: a case study at the Enfield shaker village, New Hampshire. Remote Sens. **12**(4), 690 (2020)
20. Carrio, A., Sampedro, C., Rodriguez-Ramos, A., Campoy, P.: A review of deep learning methods and applications for unmanned aerial vehicles. J. Sens. **2017**, 3296874 (2017)
21. Erdelj, M., Natalizio, E., Chowdhury, K.R., Akyildiz, I.F.: Help from the sky: leveraging UAVs for disaster management. IEEE Pervas. Comput. **16**(1), 24–32 (2017)
22. Kopardekar, P., Rios, J., Prevot, Th., Johnson, M., Jung, J., Robinson III, J.E.: Unmanned aircraft system traffic management (UTM) concept of operations. In: Proceedings of the 16th AIAA Aviation Technology, Integration, and Operations Conference, Washington, DC (2016)
23. American Red Cross. Drones for Disaster Response and Relief Operations (2015). https://www.issuelab.org/resources/21683/21683.pdf
24. Sparrow, R.: Building a better WarBot: ethical issues in the design of unmanned systems for military applications. Sci. Eng. Ethics **15**, 169–187 (2009)
25. Fotohi, R., Abdan, M., Ghasemi, S.: A self-adaptive intrusion detection system for securing UAV-to-UAV communications based on the human immune system in UAV networks. J. Grid Comput. **20**, 22 (2022). https://doi.org/10.1007/s10723-022-09614-1
26. Ayob, A.F., Arshad, M.R., Jamaludin, S., Ahmad, S.Z.A.S.: A brief review of unmanned underwater vehicle human-machine interaction. In: 2022 IEEE 9th International Conference on Underwater System Technology: Theory and Applications (USYS), Kuala Lumpur, pp. 1–4 (2022)
27. Kulik, S., Rodionov, A., Dubrovin, F., Unru, P., Mikhailenko, O.: About precision of underwater vehicles location using underwater acoustic modems. In: 2019 International Conference on Engineering and Telecommunication (EnT), Dolgoprudny, pp. 1–5 (2019)
28. Bernard, A., Al Maawali, K., Sharma, R.: Modeling of unmanned underwater vehicle with rotating thrusters for offshore rig inspection. In: 2019 1st International Conference on Unmanned Vehicle Systems-Oman (UVS), Muscat, pp. 1–6 (2019)
29. Cadena, A.: Design and construction of an autonomous underwater vehicle for the launch of a small UAV. In: 2009 IEEE International Conference on Technologies for Practical Robot Applications, Woburn, pp. 78–83 (2009)
30. Ali Shah, S.I., Khan, M., Ahmad, S.M.: Design, development, and fabrication of a low cost remotely operated unmanned underwater vehicle. In: 2021 International Conference on Robotics and Automation in Industry (ICRAI), Rawalpindi, pp. 1–5 (2021)

31. Mercado, D.A., Maia, M.M., Diez, F.J.: Aerial-underwater systems, a new paradigm in unmanned vehicles. In: 2017 International Conference on Unmanned Aircraft Systems (ICUAS), Miami, pp. 1690–1695 (2017)
32. Cheng-Qi, C., Song-Lin, Y.: Preliminary design of underwater unmanned vehicle integrated system evaluation. In: 2021 3rd International Conference on Advances in Computer Technology, Information Science and Communication (CTISC), Shanghai, pp. 1–6 (2021)
33. Kouchak, S.M., Gaffar, A.: Determinism in future cars: why autonomous trucks are easier to design. In: 2017 IEEE SmartWorld, Ubiquitous Intelligence and Computing, Advanced and Trusted Computed, Scalable Computing and Communications, Cloud and Big Data Computing, Internet of People and Smart City Innovation (SmartWorld/SCALCOM/UIC/ATC/CBDCom/IOP/SCI), San Francisco, pp. 1–6 (2017)
34. Bisht, M., Abbott, J., Gaffar, A.: Social dilemma of autonomous cars a critical analysis. In: 2017 IEEE SmartWorld, Ubiquitous Intelligence and Computing, Advanced and Trusted Computed, Scalable Computing and Communications, Cloud and Big Data Computing, Internet of People and Smart City Innovation (SmartWorld/SCALCOM/UIC/ATC/CBDCom/IOP/SCI), San Francisco, pp. 1–3 (2017)
35. Koike, A., Sueda, Y.: Contents delivery for autonomous driving cars in conjunction with car navigation system. In: 2019 20th Asia-Pacific Network Operations and Management Symposium (APNOMS), Matsue, pp. 1–4 (2019)
36. Bimbraw, K.: Autonomous cars: past, present and future a review of the developments in the last century, the present scenario and the expected future of autonomous vehicle technology. In: 2015 12th International Conference on Informatics in Control, Automation and Robotics (ICINCO), Colmar, pp. 191–198 (2015)
37. Josef Mík, A., Bouchner, B.P.: Safety of crews of autonomous cars. In: 2020 Smart City Symposium Prague (SCSP), Prague, pp. 1–5 (2020)
38. Pozna, C., Antonya, C.: Issues about autonomous cars. In: 2016 IEEE 11th International Symposium on Applied Computational Intelligence and Informatics (SACI), Timisoara, pp. 13–18 (2016)
39. Agafonov, A., Yumaganov, A.: 3D objects detection in an autonomous car driving problem. In: 2020 International Conference on Information Technology and Nanotechnology (ITNT), Samara, pp. 1–5 (2020)

Author Index

B
Borissova, Daniela   117

C
Cooper, Rodney H.   51

D
Dolchinkov, Radostin   90, 127

G
Garvanov, Ivan   17, 107
Garvanova, Gabriela   117, 136
Garvanova, Magdalena   65, 77

K
Kharakhashyan, Artem M.   33

L
Lazarov, Andon   3
Letskovska, Silvia   127

M
Maltseva, Olga A.   33
Minchev, Dimitar   3

N
Nurdaulet, Nurym   107

O
Oreshkov, Kolyo   127

P
Pergelova, Penka   107
Petersen, Brent R.   51

R
Retallick, Jeff   51

S
Seymenliyski, Kamen   127
Shishkov, Boris   77, 136
Simionov, Radoslav   127

T
Todorov, Velizar   90
Tsonkov, Georgi   65, 117

V
Ventsislavov, Kristian   90

Y
Yovkov, Atanas   90

Z
Zaerov, Eldar   127

© The Editor(s) (if applicable) and The Author(s), under exclusive license
to Springer Nature Switzerland AG 2023
B. Shishkov and A. Lazarov (Eds.): ICTRS 2023, CCIS 1990, p. 145, 2023.
https://doi.org/10.1007/978-3-031-49263-1

Printed in the United States
by Baker & Taylor Publisher Services